The Best Is Yet To Be

The Memoirs of
Vern Heidebrecht

Mill Lake Books

Judson Lake House
PUBLISHERS

Mill Lake Books
An imprint of Judson Lake House Publishers
30885 Polar Avenue
Abbotsford, B.C. V4X 1Y8
Canada
www.judsonlakehouse.com

Front cover photo courtesy of The Abbotsford News.
Cover design and layout by Daniel Doucette.
Chapter illustrations by Sheila Kent.
Editing by James R. Coggins, Abbotsford, B.C. www.coggins.ca

ISBN 978-0-9881462-0-4

Dedication

This book is dedicated to my family—to my wife, Carol, who has lived for most of my life alongside me, and also to my children and grandchildren: Murray and Holly and their children Noah and Avery; Bob and JoAnn and their children Karis, Connor, and Elisa; Dave and Michelle and their children, Jonas, Jack, and Jase; and Karla and Menno and their children, Karli, Riley, Maya, and Brody. These are the most important people in my life!

November 2004

Acknowledgements

This book would not have come into existence without the incredible help and encouragement of my sister, Agnes Ratzlaff.

I would also like to give thanks to my editor, Jim Coggins, for his skillful direction and encouragement; to Hilda Hildebrand for her hours of tireless typing; and to Sheila Kent, who came alongside just when we needed her with her artistic expertise and counsel. Thank you to Ruth Sherk, Tom Reimer, Susan Anquist, Garry Schmidt, and my wife, Carol, for reading the manuscript and offering valuable input. Thank you, also, to my son, Dave, who regularly checked up with "How's it going, Dad?" and to the many friends who have encouraged me to continue when it would have been easier to give up.

My hope has always been..."The best is yet to be!"

Agnes and Vern

Table of Contents

Introduction

"The best is yet to be."
Robert Browning

"Whatever you do, do it all to the glory of God."
1 Corinthians 10:31

"And we know that in all things God works for the good of those who love him, who have been called according to his purpose."
Romans 8:28

The dictionary defines "memoir" as a written account of one's life. This book is a dip into the memory bank of my life, the memory bank of myself and my wife, Carol. Together, we have experienced God's grace and goodness.

About ten years ago, I was diagnosed with Parkinson's disease, a progressive neurological disorder. It was somewhat comforting to become aware that people such as Billy Graham, Muhammad Ali, Pope John Paul II, and Michael J. Fox have also dealt with this disease.

Michael J. Fox has become world renowned in leading the battle against Parkinson's through funding research and writing. Fox demonstrates a positive attitude that I have sought to emulate. His best seller *Always Looking Up: The Adventures of an Incurable Optimist* gives insights into how to deal with the difficulties and tests that we encounter in life.

Robert Browning, the renowned poet, picks up this theme in his poem "Rabbi Ben Ezra," inviting us to plan for the best:

Grow old along with me!
The best is yet to be . . .
Our times are in His hand
Who saith, 'A whole I planned,
Youth shows but half; trust God: see all nor be afraid!'

There are three reasons why I am sharing these stories and reflections with you:

First, for the glory of God. The Scriptures encourage us, "Whatever you do, do it all to the glory of God" (1 Corinthians 10:31). When my children and their children read this account, my prayer is that they will see the marvels of God's glory in the events of my life.

Second, to demonstrate the truth of Romans 8:28: "And we know that in all things God works for the good of those who love him, who have been called according to his purpose." This is an amazing declaration that "all things" work together for something good. In these stories I am telling, the fingerprints of God are evident everywhere.

Third, to give evidence of God's grace. In 2 Corinthians 12:9, God promises, "My grace is sufficient for you, for my power is made perfect in weakness." This has been my life verse for most of my forty-three years of ministry. I want to bear witness to the fact that God teaches us and enables us to celebrate and grow in every situation if we constantly lean on Him and His direction.

I invite you to read and be encouraged in your spiritual journey.

Chapter 1
Celebrating My Roots

"The heavens are opened in my heart."
Old German hymn

It was a bitterly cold February day. The snow dump had been unexpected, and the wind was causing severe drifting. The young couple found themselves in a quandary. Katie was pregnant and already in labor pains. The plan had been to bring her to Edmonton, where a very modern hospital facility could offer every assistance she would need to deliver her child. It was not to be. It was too far to drive in the precarious weather, especially for a woman in her condition.

Grandma Margaretha Heidebrecht was there to help her daughter-in-law through this time of birthing. David, the husband, was nervously trudging about the house wondering what to do next. He had already been down the road to use his neighbor's telephone to call Dr. Law and let him know that he was desperately needed in the Heidebrecht household. But he was not showing up!

David kept feeding the little potbellied stove with wood and made sure that the gas lamp was shining as brightly as possible. It was not supposed to be happening this way. He had no experience in helping to birth a child. He was very uneasy about the whole situation.

Finally he said to his wife, Katie, "I'm going to saddle up my horse and look for the doctor. We need him here now!" The truth was, he didn't feel he'd be of much use when the baby was being born. He had a sensitive spot when it came to young mothers. His own mother had died two years after David was born. So he wanted to provide real help during this critical time in their lives.

After he left, Grandma tried peering out the window to see if help was coming, but the glass was frozen with ice and condensation. She took a warm cloth and tried to wipe some of the ice off so she could see more clearly. Someone had to be coming soon. She was not very experienced as a midwife, and she was praying and anticipating that the good Lord would help. She wanted to be the first to see the doctor coming.

After what seemed like an eternity but was in reality closer to an hour, she thought she saw a light in the distant roadway. Could someone be coming? The birth pains were closer together and more intense. Grandma tried to encourage her daughter-in-law as well as she knew how.

She went back to the window again and thought she saw some movement down the road. Was it a horse with a rider on it? Or was she just seeing things? She announced the possible sighting to her daughter-in-law, and there was a brief smile.

Sure enough, it was not only the doctor on his horse, but also David, who was riding on his own steed on their way to the little house on the prairie. They entered the cabin, stomping their boots to clear the snow. The doctor asked David to take his own horse as well as David's and feed him in the barn. David was delighted to get out of the house and let the doctor take care of matters. It was cold, but David hardly felt it. His heart was pounding, and he felt a great sense of anticipation that another child would be born into his family. When David heard the cry of a newborn child, he quickened his steps and ran into the house—where he was pleased to discover that his wife had given birth to a son. As the child was being washed, Katie dedicated this child to the ministry. Only the years to come would tell the whole story. This was really a gift from God.

The doctor enquired, "What shall we name the young man?"

Now David broke in and shared the insight that they had received several weeks earlier while they had talked about naming the child. "We'll name him Werner." They had some German neighbors with this name, and they had decided they would use it if they should have a son.

Dr. Law smiled, seeing that everything was now in good order. And that is how the child born to David and Katie Heidebrecht on February 24, 1941 was named Werner; later my name was shortened to Vern. There may have been a war going on elsewhere in the world, but there was joy in this household.

Deeper Roots

My father, David Heidebrecht, had been born into a Mennonite home in Hamburg, Molotschna, the Ukraine. Much of what I know about my ancestors is told in my grandparents' biography, *Thy Grace is Sufficient: The David A. and Margaretha Heidebrecht Story.*

The Mennonites had been invited into the Ukraine by Catherine the Great of Russia. She had in mind that people who knew agrarian science and engineering were needed to help bring the Russian economy up to par with the rest of the world. Everything went fine for the Mennonites until the communists took over in 1918. The result was that by early 1928 Mennonites of every socio-economic class were characterized as "enemies of the state" and subject to high taxes and expropriation of their property, including their unharvested crops. To keep the pressure up, the government enacted new laws which restricted their religious observances. The laws forbade the teaching of the Christian faith to children in the schools, limited the public observation of worship services on Sunday and religious holidays, and significantly increased taxes on church buildings. When the Mennonites failed to pay the taxes or broke one of the new laws, their church buildings were expropriated and converted into community halls, sports facilities, and barns. Beyond the legal issues, "all hell broke loose" in the local communities, as the communists stole livestock from the farmers, raped the women, and destroyed agrarian life.

The result was that many Mennonites moved to Siberia, believing that if they were no longer near the center of the Soviet empire, they would be able to make a fair living. Among them were David and Margaretha Heidebrecht, and their family, including young David, my father. (My grandfather, David, had married Margaretha following the death of his first wife, Anna.) Following the "call of the north," they moved first to the colony of Neu-Samara and then on to Siberia. However, things only got progressively worse.

The most obvious way to avoid persecution was to immigrate to North America. From 1923 to early 1927, over 17,000 Mennonites left the Soviet Union and arrived in Canada. Hoping to join the exodus, my grandparents and two other couples determined to go by rail all the way from Siberia to Moscow. This was not a comfortable ride. They leased a box car and used it as transportation all the way to Moscow. The container was drafty, the weather was cold, and the amenities were at a bare minimum. They ate roasted buns and warmed up soup in containers beside the railway track whenever the train stopped to pick up passengers and wares.

When they finally got to Moscow, the couples rented a house on the outskirts of the city. Each of the three families was able to rent only one room, so these were tight quarters indeed. They remained in this situation for six months. Daily, they went to the office where visas could be obtained, with no success at all. They were told they should go back to their home village and stay there because no more visas would be issued and they would not be allowed to leave Russia and immigrate to Canada.

Young David, my father, was not a Christian. He had enjoyed his life of being in the center of the action and running with the crowd in his village. But during this time of intense danger and waiting for a miracle to bring the family to Canada, he began to pray. He did not pray to receive Christ into his life; rather, he prayed that they would be able to escape Russia. It was two years after they arrived in Canada when he finally surrendered his life to the Lord. It took place just before evangelistic meetings were to be held in their area. Late one evening, at 11:00 p.m., he was in the middle of a deep struggle. He recalled, "I woke my father, and he prayed with me. I could not open my mouth for prayer. With the help of my father, the breakthrough finally came in the morning while I was doing chores. I placed my faith in Christ and was sure He had accepted me."

Back in Moscow, the Mennonites were still hoping to leave the Soviet Union. The story which follows is told in more detail in the book *Reminiscences from the Lives of Peter and Anna Epp.* A friend, Peter Froese, advised my grandparents and two other families wishing to emigrate to apply for a hearing before an official named Tovarisch Smidowitsch. He had had a good connection with Peter Froese in the past, so they went to ask for his help in obtaining the required documents. To their surprise, their request was granted. It was a miracle. Meanwhile, thousands of Mennonites and Germanic people from across the Soviet Union were gathering in Moscow to obtain similar visas. However, the government absolutely refused to make more available. An official said that visas were being granted on a limited basis only for the sixty to seventy people who had first come to Moscow and made their application. It was a sad day for those who could not immigrate to Canada, but it was a joyful celebration for those who had the opportunity to finally make this life-changing move.

It was July 1929. My grandparents and their family got ready and made their way to Leningrad, by ship to England, and then again by ship to Quebec. One thing they remembered clearly was the abundance of food on the ship. They were not used to having this kind of bountiful fare on their tables. They felt like royalty. From Quebec City, they went by train all the way to Edmonton, Alberta, and from there they came down to the town of Tofield.

The immigrants had a lot to think about. They were in a new country and were totally unfamiliar with its customs. They didn't know the language or the methods of doing business. The Lord would have to help them make it in this new situation. The Stutzman family had sponsored my grandparents and their family with the funds necessary to bring them across the ocean to Canada. My Dad told me that on the first day of their arrival they got organized and on the second day they were in the bush chopping wood, earning twenty-five cents an hour. But they were so pleased and thankful to be out of the communist system and to have a new beginning in Canada. They even remember the first lunch they received during their wood chopping responsibilities: a cooked potato with the peel still on, an egg with salt and pepper, cold coffee, and a piece of meat. Their means were small, but their dreams were big. The Lord had given them another chance to develop a faith community and serve Him.

New Roots in a New Land

My father, David, was eighteen years old when he arrived in Canada, and he worked at various jobs in order to make a living. Later, he qualified under the homestead land act, which was designed to help populate new areas of the West. The applicant had to be at least eighteen years old and be industrious enough to clear and cultivate at least fifty-five of the granted 160 acres of land in the first five years of its occupancy. Dad's property, NE-51-20-W-4, was hilly and covered with a heavy growth of bush and deciduous trees of considerable girth.

David began to get serious about looking for a wife after he had secured this property for his future family. His father was a minister, who often traveled throughout the province of Alberta and thus met people who could give good information regarding eligible mates for marriage. In this way, David heard about a young woman who lived in Calgary and was working as a housemaid for a Jewish family. He liked the description of this young lady which he had heard from his father, so he wrote her a letter. Katie Martens, the one who received the letter, was totally surprised that someone would reach out to her in this way. The next day, she received a dozen roses from her suitor. They met twice, and, after some struggle, they agreed that they loved one another and wanted to be married. The great event took place November 13, 1937. They made their home in Lindbrook, Alberta.

Now this hard-working Heidebrecht began preparing a home for his new wife and the family they anticipated. He rented a gas-driven motorized sawmill, which he used to mill lumber from the bush trees that were biggest in size. He built a house, twenty-four feet by twelve feet. It was a simple house with two windows and only one room. It was heated by a wood stove. There was no telephone, running water, or inside toilet.

One thing I remember about that house is that later on, behind the house, was Grandma's big garden. We kids enjoyed pulling carrots, shucking peas, and eating the wide variety of vegetables she grew there. Dad had also planted a row of chokecherry trees next to the house. The taste was tart but inviting, and Rosa, my older sister, and I spent hours enjoying the sharp flavor!

Dad also built a cow barn. He milked three to five cows and separated the cream from the rest of the milk. The cream was cooled and sold to the creamery in Tofield. It was one way of bringing in some cash for developing the farm.

I remember a funny incident that happened in the cow barn. It was always difficult to milk a cow for the first time. My Dad became rather impatient with one cow and put kickers on the cow's back feet. This made it impossible for the cow to kick and knock the milk pail out of my father's hands. He finally did get some milk from the cow and then released her from the station into the barnyard. It was only then that he realized he had forgotten to take the kickers off the cow. You should have seen that cow jump with the kickers remaining on her back legs. It was almost like the nursery rhyme: "Hey diddle diddle, the cat and the fiddle, the cow jumped over the moon!"

Dad also built a chicken barn. He specialized in "hatching eggs." We had to bring the eggs into Edmonton, where they were hatched and sold to various farmers. I recall another unique occurrence. One day while Dad was gathering eggs in the chicken barn, he spotted a skunk helping himself to the eggs. Dad tried to chase the skunk out of the chicken barn, but the skunk got the draw on him and squirted him liberally. When Dad got into the house, Mom chased him out. She wouldn't have anything to do with the leftover smell from that terrible skunk. She wouldn't wash the clothes or try to recoup the loss. She insisted that they dig a hole and bury the skunk-perfumed clothes. He obeyed. Even so, it took days to get the smell out of our house.

A sad day came when our dog, Sport, had a run-in with a porcupine. He was in great pain, and there was no way we could help him. It was sad, but Dad had to put the dog down. Of course, we weren't allowed to be near when this act of mercy was accomplished.

A high time in the farm community was threshing time. I recall about seven farmers coming with their teams of horses and wagons into our wheat fields, which had already been harvested and stooked. There was a huge steam-driven tractor, from which a drive belt was hooked to the threshing machine. When everything was lined up, the switch was turned on to make everything work. It was exciting and noisy.

I begged my dad to let me have some kind of job on the threshing crew. He finally put me into the granary. As the wheat was augured into the granary, I had the job of keeping the grain level so it wouldn't get too high in any one corner. I also recall sitting on a wagonload of wheat stalks and hearing my Dad say that our two horses, Bill and Tom, were the best in the whole lot. I was proud to sit beside my dad and enjoy this highlight of harvesting.

We had a big hole dug in the side of our yard. When the winter snows blew and the ice was thick, Dad would take the horse and sled, cut huge chunks of ice out of the pond, and put them on the sled. He would then drop them into the big hole in the yard. This usually took several days. When the hole was full, we covered the top with a canvas sheet and sawdust. This became an excellent place to store our can of cream while it was waiting to be picked up each week, and we also had ice available for making ice cream and other delectables in the heat of summer.

My older sister, Rosa, and I enjoyed the farm and the many opportunities to experiment and try new things. She and I were walking by a swamp one day when we happened to spy an ax head. I picked it up, and she dared me to throw it into the water. I hesitated because I thought Dad might want to use that ax head for his work on the farm. However, being dared to do so, I threw it into the pond. After this, Rosa looked at me and said, "I'm going to tell Dad, I'm going to tell Dad!" From that day on until I was about eight years old, whenever I threatened to report something that she had done, she would remind me of the ax head that I had thrown away, knowing that I would certainly be spanked for it if Dad knew.

A third child came into our family, Agnes, and then a fourth, George. I recall George coming home from the hospital with Grandma and me being excited that I would have a brother to grow up with. Agnes proved to be a warm, gentle, serving sister. I enjoyed my siblings a lot.

The one-room house on the prairie was too limited for a family of six, so Dad built a house with an upstairs and more square footage. I recall that when the construction was underway, there was scaffolding alongside the roof about ten feet off the ground. Rosa and I were busily sticking the leftover pieces of shingles between the shingles already installed on the roof and then pulling them out again and throwing them onto the ground. Rosa, however, pulled so hard she lost her balance on the scaffolding and had a long fall to the ground. She couldn't breathe, and we were afraid she might have broken her back. However, by God's grace, she recovered. She was a tough girl.

Light Breaks Through

Sundays were important in the pioneer days. We went to church by wagon in summer and by sleigh in winter. In winter, we would heat bricks and put them under our feet to keep us somewhat warm on the journey to church. Mom and Dad lived the closest to the church in Lindbrook, and so they got there an hour earlier than everyone else and made sure the wood furnace was blasting out heat to make the facility warm.

Several clear memories have stayed with me from that place of worship. First, I recall having my pocket full of marbles and sitting near the front of the church. Children customarily sat near the front to listen; there was no Sunday school in that church. In any case, I put my hand into my pocket and began looking at the marbles during the service. I lost control, and the whole pocketful of marbles rolled to the front of the church. Everything became quiet, including the minister. I received a reminder of what I should do in church and what I shouldn't be involved in, in the form of a spanking from my father, following the service.

Another, similar event happened the Sunday I received a stick of gum from a friend of mine. I had never had gum in my mouth before. I enjoyed smacking my lips and chewing rather exaggeratedly in the front row of the church auditorium. I remember that when the service was over, the minister was on my heels and gave me some stern warnings about chewing gum in church while he was trying to preach.

I also recall a certain Sunday when we were singing a German song which said (in English): "The heavens are opened in my heart. Do you know why? Because Jesus died and suffered for us." The moment we sang "The heavens are opened," the clouds parted in the sky, and a brilliant sun shone in through the windows of the church. I was startled. It seemed as if the heavens had indeed been opened the very moment we sang that phrase from the German song. I said to myself, "There is a God!"

Church was an exciting event. After the service was over, we opened our lunchboxes and ate a sumptuous meal together. As a five-year-old, I skipped from family to family and chose the best each had to offer. After all, young kids were cute and deserved the best! At least, that was the feeling that I had as I did my best to get the best from each person who had brought a lunch to the service.

Now, unexpectedly, in the fall of 1946, there was talk about moving to British Columbia. It was disconcerting to find myself thinking about leaving this place that was familiar and enjoyable and that was where my grandma and grandpa lived. However, when Dad said it was time to move, we moved.

I knew things would be new, but the best was yet to be.

Chapter 2
Growing from First Grade to Eighth Grade

"Finish your outdoor work and get your fields ready;
after that, build your house."
Proverbs 24:27

My father had gone on ahead to British Columbia in order to scout out a place for the family to live. Meanwhile, Mom had to make her way to British Columbia with four children on her hands. I recall distinctly being on the railway train and causing Mom no end of consternation. We would run up and down the aisles and bump into the people who were serving. She finally convinced us that the conductor, who had that distinctive hat, was really a policeman—and that the next time we would be caught, we would be put into the train jail. That slowed us down—for an hour or two at least.

When we finally arrived in Chilliwack, B.C., our good friends from Matsqui, Joe and Rosa Susbauer, along with my dad, were there with their car to pick us up. It was the Christmas season. We had a small

Christmas party in a hotel in Chilliwack at which we exchanged gifts. I received a small carpenter's apron with a hammer and some nail packs. I recall swallowing one of the tacks and the fear the doctor had that I might puncture my innards in some way. But it all worked out, and I'm still living.

The Susbauers then drove us to the farm on Marshall Road which my Dad had purchased in what is now Abbotsford. Finally we got an opportunity to see the farm. It was twenty-two and a half acres of property. The house was small, with a very small bedroom downstairs and two small bedrooms upstairs. There was a small barn big enough for four or five milk cows. Otherwise, it was a very simple piece of property with very few outbuildings. One thing Dad made clear to us was that we needed to clear twenty acres of property to make the farm pay for itself. This would be a big job. But he had the hope that "the best was yet to be."

One way of looking at my first years in British Columbia is to focus on my schooling and to point out the teachers and the events that related to my experience with them.

Mrs. Kerr: Grade One

School was a new experience for me. I had not had any kindergarten to prepare me for grade one, and I was used to speaking German, not English.

The one thing that stands out distinctly in my mind is how the class was broken into reading groups. First there were the bluebirds (the best readers), next there were the robins (the second best), and last there were the blackbirds. I began in the blackbird category and worked my way up to being a robin. I recall distinctly how embarrassed I felt that I couldn't do better and be at the top of the class. But it was a good year, and we had a good teacher.

The school was called North Poplar. The school building was old but good. There was a potbellied stove that we needed to add wood to several times a day, and there were outside privies for bathrooms. Behind the school were two to three acres of bush land. Every recess, we would go roaring down the wild trail that had been marked out for kids to play on. It was a grand adventure. Imaginations would run wild.

There was a store at the corner of Marshall Road and Clearbrook Road called the Ellis store; today the location is buried under the intersection where Clearbrook Road and Number 1 Highway meet. What I enjoyed buying most was jawbreakers, three for a penny.

Most of the other kids had nice lunch pails and a very Canadian type of sandwich for the noon hour. We had a syrup pail and homemade bread sandwiches. We didn't quite fit in with the rest of the kids in the school. But grade one was still a good year.

Miss Hickey: Grade Two

Grade two was also at North Poplar School. What I remember most clearly from this year was that I had a teacher who wore lipstick. I had never seen my mother wear anything of the sort, and I was mesmerized by the fact that my teacher wore lipstick. I think I was in love with her. But grade two was a good learning year. I was catching on to English and enjoyed taking books home from the church library and reading quite a bit.

Mrs. Keller: Grade Three

Mrs. Keller was a First Nations woman. She was very easy on us as students, and we got away with quite a bit. I recall a prank I pulled to protect myself in times when I hadn't done my homework. She would go up and down each row, and we'd all have to give an answer to a question. When it got close to being my turn, I would put my head down and whack my nose with my knuckle. It never failed to draw blood. So I could go out and be in the hallway with a bloody nose when it was my turn to answer a question. But that was the only year I could get by with that kind of behavior. It actually put me behind in reading and math skills.

Mrs. Doerksen: Grade Four

Schools in the Lower Mainland area were all full, so they carted a number of us to the Abbotsford Airport barracks to be educated. We had a lot of fun watching the airplanes and enjoying the unique things at this location. Mrs. Doerksen was a good teacher. She helped me catch up on many skills from grade three.

When I was pastoring in Abbotsford at about age fifty, Mrs. Doerksen came to one of the Christmas programs at our church, and we chatted. She remembered me, and had many good things to say. It was exciting to bump into someone from that far back and be affirmed.

One thing that I experienced as a youngster was when my dad took me aside and said I needed to take some responsibility to help make the farm work. So he taught me how to milk a cow, feed the cattle, and gather eggs at the hen house. It also meant that when he was out of town working in his construction business, I would often have to stay home on a school day and do the chores that he hadn't been there to take care of. Because of this, I did lag behind in school from time to time.

Mrs. Ellis: Grade Five

I was back at North Poplar School the next year. Mrs. Ellis was a fascinating teacher. She and her husband had been in the diplomatic corps, working in China. They had experienced revolutions and many other interesting things in that faraway land. Her delight was to read to us as a class a chapter a day from the Bible, as well as to read to us other books from her wide range of experience. She was a strict but good teacher.

Mrs. Ellis: Grade Six

It was fun being in the oldest class at the school. It meant I could be on the school softball team, football team, and track team. I do recall that I had a few run-ins with other students and several wrestling matches. Looking back, I think it is part of a young man's growing up experience to lock horns with someone and tussle with them. At least, that's what it looks like from where I'm sitting today.

I remember that Mrs. Ellis got upset with me in class on one occasion, called me to the front of the class, and smacked my hand with a ruler. It didn't hurt a bit, but I still remember the blush I had on my face as a result of being publicly disciplined.

Mr. Craven: Grade Seven

This was an exciting year for me because we were leaving the small country school and going to a big city school. Abbotsford Junior High School was newly built, and we were the first ones to use it.

Mr. Craven was in his first teaching assignment. I can still repeat almost verbatim some of the lessons he taught the first few weeks. It was very interesting, and he did a very good job of explaining the content.

Each class had to have a representative to serve on the junior high student council. Because Mr. Craven liked me, I think he campaigned for me, and I was elected representative of our class. I recall one of the responsibilities was to give a speech in front of the whole student body on behalf of our class. I did it, but I think I must have lost several pounds of sweat carrying out that assignment. But grade seven was a good year.

Again, years later, after I moved back to Abbotsford as an adult in 1988, I bumped into Mr. Craven on the sidewalk going for a bite to eat at a local restaurant. We had a delightful conversation, and we both had positive memories of those first few years of his teaching career.

Miss Viola Doerksen (Ratzlaff): Grade Eight

Viola was a first-year teacher at Mennonite Educational Institute, where I attended grade eight. She was an interesting teacher and took time for the students. Later I found out that she had had no preparation time for the classes that were assigned to her last minute and she had to work almost day and night to keep up with her work as a teacher. But she was a good instructor, and I enjoyed the year.

German School

An added requirement in our Mennonite community was that we were expected to learn how to read and write German. So, on Saturdays, we would trudge off to our church and take German school in the morning. It really wasn't that exciting or much fun. The teachers weren't very well equipped for the job at times either. Some of them had left the barn just hours before they came into the classroom—and their shoes showed it.

The annual closing program for the German school was always a bit of a difficult experience for those of us who weren't that good in German. We had to write from memory a German verse and also practice "schoeneschrift" (neat penmanship).

Farm Life

On the farm on which we lived, we had two ponds, which usually froze over in the winter, and we enjoyed having delightful skating events there and playing hockey.

Meanwhile, our farm was developing, and Dad had the courage to try various new ventures. One of them was to buy a tractor. I'll never forget that day! I was in grade two when he came home with the tractor. I still know what it smelled like, what it sounded like, and the power that it had. It was such an exciting thing to be able to do work in the farmyard with the tractor. When I was in grade six, I learned how to cut hay. So, I did that for Dad, and I also hired myself out to do it for my neighbors. Today, when I drive down some of the roads near my former home, I can point out the fields where I once mowed hay. Today, those fields are full of houses.

My dad liked the verse in Proverbs that said build your barns first and after that build your homes (Proverbs 24:27). He had taken that priority to heart on our first farm in Lindbrook, Alberta, and was doing the same here. Our house was small, drafty, and highly inadequate for our family. When I was twelve years old, another child entered our family, Ruth. Now there were Ruth, Rosa, and Agnes in one room upstairs and my brother, George, and me in the other room. There were two serious limitations in that house. First, we had no running hot water. So, Saturday was literally bath night. Everyone would take a bath in a tub we pulled into the kitchen—and the dirtier you were, the later in the line-up you came. That meant that the girls always bathed first, and I knew I would almost always be last. The second limitation was that, because there was no indoor plumbing, we had to go to an outhouse to take care of business. It was very uncomfortable on a cold wintry day or a rainy summer day. So, it was time to build a new house. But, true to Dad's value system, we built the barn first.

It was not to be an ordinary barn, but a special barn. It would be a barn with a round roof. The most demanding thing we had to do in making this building was to shape the rafters. In the evenings, after chores, my Dad and I would cut board after board to the right measurements for this roof. When it was done, we had an attractive barn with a roof that was unique. I had been part of the process of construction from laying the concrete to shingling the roof. I recall that we had a visitor from out of town at our home on one occasion and I explained to him how we had built the barn. Larry remarked to my dad, "It sounds like Vern did the whole thing by himself." I was somewhat embarrassed, yet I felt I had had a significant part in building it, and I took ownership of it. When this new barn was done, we could milk sixteen cows. We also purchased a milking machine. I had helped milk by hand our five cows in the small barn. It was exciting to enter the 20th century in milk production and use a modern machine to do the job with much greater speed and a new degree of cleanliness.

Then there was the "picking" season. Cash crops were excellent opportunities to teach us young people how to work and earn some money. When I was in grade six and seven in particular, I worked the crop picking circuit in our community.

Strawberry picking always came first. You had to crawl on the ground to pick the berries. We often had strawberry fights to ease the boredom. The first year we planted strawberries, we had an unusually large bumper crop. It brought some much needed revenue into Dad's pocket to care for a family of five children.

Next came raspberry season. Most of us went to pick raspberries somewhere in the Fraser Valley. It was the thing to do. About the time I was in grades seven and eight, Rosa and I joined a troop of pickers at Abe Martens's place near the village of Yarrow. There were about eight girls, and I was the lone boy in the picking team. The girls were housed for the night in a converted barn, and I stayed overnight in a small chicken barn. I tried my hand at cooking, and they did the same. It was an interesting part of the picking circuit.

The next crop to be picked was beans. This proved to be very boring, compared to picking other produce.

More exciting was the picking of hops. This happened in Chilliwack about twenty-five miles from where we lived. We were picked up by a truck at six in the morning, and our whole family was involved in the work. We always told people that we picked hops that would go to make yeast, not beer. When I was fifteen, I got a job working in the hops kilns, a job where I was paid the same rate as an adult. I was proud of that and tried to impress my boss continually.

Growing the Farm

Every year, my father would stake out three to four acres of our property that he planned to clear and bring under cultivation. This was an adventurous time because it meant we would be blasting stumps. The stumps were heavy and up to eight feet in diameter. In 1929, the logs had been harvested from this particular property, and most of them had found their way to San Francisco, where they were used in rebuilding the city after the great earthquake. Now we had the stumps and bush to contend with. The job involved digging a hole under the root system of a stump with a small shovel, then filling the hole with three or four sticks of blasting powder and a blasting cap. The fuse was connected, and enough length was allowed so the person who lit the fuse could run away to a safe distance after it was ignited. And run we did—and then waited for the blast to occur. We would carefully hide ourselves behind big stumps so we would be protected. When the blast occurred, it was always something of an adventure. Then came the tedious work of picking up the roots, stones, and other debris. Many a Saturday we children spent the day picking up roots and doing the other work necessary to bring the property under cultivation.

The first crop of hay or berries grown on the property cleared in this way was absolutely amazing. The years of mulch that had accumulated on the surface of the soil had enriched it greatly.

In any spare time that Dad and we kids could find, we began the process of building the new house. It reminded me very much of what we had done in Alberta. We had first had our little twelve by fourteen-foot shed in Alberta and then built a two-story house. Now we were going to do it all over again. We started digging the basement by hand with a shovel, but we soon found it to be too arduous a task, and so we got a scoop that we could hitch behind the tractor in order to dig a trench for the foundation. After the house was framed, Mother convinced Dad that we needed to build a bathroom in this house before we did anything else. So we undertook the task of putting in the fixtures, together with the hot water heater and all the amenities that go into a modern bathroom. We could hardly believe that we had something as modern and convenient as that room. So, we would find ourselves taking our shower and then running across the yard to our old house to sleep. Eventually, however, we got the house completed.

The Value of Family

My siblings were a significant part of my growing up years on the farm. Rosa was always there getting involved in wanting to help. Something dramatic would always happen when she came by. Either you would be sloshed by a pail of water or you would be tickled energetically.

My next sister, Agnes, was kind of the philosopher. She had the gift of helps. Cleaning and polishing my shoes was not above her. Listening and loving were her style.

George was the brother I loved to work with. He could work without speaking much for a whole day. But I would love working with his presence beside me. He became the outstanding athlete of the family.

Ruth, who came into our family later, was the poet laureate in our family. She could write, sing, and entertain us. She became a real encouragement to Dad and Mom as well, since she remained home longer than the rest of us. Later, Ruth had wide experience of traveling and undertaking a great variety of jobs.

Spiritual Developments

My spiritual life was well grounded. I had learned the Bible ever since I was a child, and I loved Jesus. As a matter of fact, I can't think of a time that I didn't love Jesus. It surprised me, therefore, when I was seven years old, that I began to realize that I needed to also open up my life and accept Jesus as my Savior. We had an evangelist come to our church, who explained that to us. All who wanted to make this decision were to come forward, and he would pray with them. I felt insecure about that. For this reason, the next day at home, I surprised my mother by asking her if she would help me become a believer. She quickly took the big German family Bible and ushered me upstairs to my room, where she read John 3:16 to me in German.

Then she told me what it meant to be a Christian. She coached me with the words to say to invite Christ into my life. It was an exciting moment. I felt renewed.

The next morning, when Dad came in from chores, it was obvious that Mom had had a conversation with him. He took me in his arms and sat me on his lap. Then he asked me what I had done the previous night. I told him that I'd invited Jesus into my life. He squeezed me in his arms, and there was a tear in his eye. I don't think I had ever felt closer to my dad than at that moment. Interestingly enough, from that point on, I had a latent interest in telling people about Jesus. As a matter of fact, I was already thinking then about being a pastor.

I had made that commitment to Christ when I was seven years old. I was excited about that experience, and spoke to my friends about Jesus on the way home from school. I think I shocked some of them when I did this, but they paid some attention.

But, as the years went on, when I was about age twelve or thirteen, I began to doubt whether I really was a Christian. One of the reasons was that when my dad would discipline me, he would use a line something like, "And you call yourself a Christian!?" I knew Christians weren't supposed to do what I was doing. It might be talking back, disobeying, or not being truthful—but I found myself struggling with not being a perfect person. Finally, when I was fifteen years old, I no longer considered myself a Christian. No one could struggle with doing wrong things as much as I did and still be a Christian. My mother would come and want to pray with me at night, but I would simply turn over in bed, not face her, and be quiet.

It was also the Elvis Presley age, so we had our ducktails and long sideburns, and an attitude to match. Later on, I'll tell you how, by God's grace, I finally made my way through this time in my life.

But, all in all, the grades one through eight years were times of rich experiences, frustrations, and adventures. The Lord was with me, and He was doing things in my life which I was only sensing from a distance. And it was good to be part of our family. But the best was yet to be.

Chapter 3
The Exciting Teenage Years

"How much better to get wisdom than gold,
to choose understanding rather than silver!"
Proverbs 16:16

I see grades nine to thirteen as a special season of my life. As I reflect back, I see how God used many influences in that season to lay a foundation for the rest of my life. I entered these years very insecure about myself and the future, and exited those times with a compass set for the rest of my life. A phrase that I often used, and often had parroted back to me, was, "Wouldn't it be great!" In other words, I was enthusiastic about the future and saw greatness as a real possibility—greatness in the sense that I wanted to live life to its fullest.

Again, I felt it would be helpful to organize this chapter around the teachers that I had as homeroom instructors during my high school years—and include some anecdotes that would demonstrate how each teacher made a unique impact on my life.

Bill A. Wiebe: Principal

Mr. Wiebe was principal of Mennonite Educational Institute in Clearbrook (now part of Abbotsford), a teacher of math, and a no-nonsense type of instructor. We dared not enter his class without having our homework done. But he also was a man who had great faith in his students and sought to help us along in our journey. I especially remember when he came to me at the beginning of grade thirteen and asked if I would coach the junior varsity basketball team. I was first string on the senior varsity team at that time, and the school didn't have an instructor to do this, so he asked if I would do it. I said, "Yes!"

It was an exciting winter of basketball. We not only won some games, but we won the Fraser Valley championship. That same group of basketball stars went on, as the varsity team, to win the British Columbia high school championship—and did so with style. It's exciting to look back and realize that I was coaching my brother, George, who was named the Most Valuable Player in the province, and my future brother-in-law, Dan Ratzlaff, who was an outstanding player. I realized how much I enjoyed motivating people to do well, play hard, and share the pain and the glory with a team that wins.

John Ratzlaff: Grade Nine

Mr. Ratzlaff taught us biology and music, and he also took a personal interest in me as a student. He invited us to his house to help him do some concrete work. It felt good to get to know a teacher one-on-one in a relaxed setting.

Mr. Ratzlaff also took our class on a mountain climbing hike looking for Lost Lake on Sumas Mountain. Everything went well until I fell and tore open my knee. It took about five hours until people with the right equipment could get up to where I was and carry me to the ambulance and then transport me to emergency care at the Abbotsford hospital. Two surgeries later, I was able to walk again and work out some of the frustrations that I had felt because of the two-week layover in the hospital. But, praise God, everything went well in the end. John Ratzlaff was a very significant influence on my life.

Eric Ratzlaff: Grade Ten

Eric Ratzlaff taught us church history and German. He had a sharp temper, and it was often felt when his students were not behaving. A typical punishment was to send a student out of the class to the principal's office.

My most memorable encounter with Eric Ratzlaff was when I was doing some schoolwork one day and I asked him whether he thought I had the capacity to improve my grades enough to finish high school. He said that he had his doubts, but that I could do well as a farmer. I'll never forget the feeling I had, that I wasn't smart enough to finish high school. Years later, when I finished my doctorate, I realized that the way he had spoken to me had influenced me to work hard and not only finish my high school, but also finish a few grades after that. He was used by the Lord to motivate me, in a negative way, but the result was positive.

Jacob Toews: Grade Eleven

Jacob Toews taught English and German. He was the kind of teacher who was thorough, but could make fifteen minutes seem like two hours. More than once in his class I had to stir myself back to alertness, so I could catch on to what was being taught and be able to answer the next question. Diagramming sentences and analyzing poetry were not my first love. However, he taught basic English skills, which helped me in my school work later on in university and graduate school. He had a good impact on my life.

William Neufeld: Grade Twelve

Mr. Neufeld taught English literature and languages and made English come alive, especially the stories by classic writers. I greatly anticipated his classes and enjoyed reading the books he assigned. He was also an artist. When I finished writing my first book, I called him. He had forgotten my name, but I was able to thank him for the help he had been to me in my school years.

C.D. Toews: Grade Thirteen

C.D. Toews was our instructor in choral singing and men's chorus. I was a member of an award-winning men's chorus. It was not that I could sing well, but I always made sure I stood next to someone who held the tenor line well. We had a lot of fun traveling, singing, and winning contests due to the good singers in our group.

I had many other good and valuable instructors, but the ones I have mentioned were my homeroom teachers, who made a direct impact on me from day to day—and I am grateful.

As I have reflected on my high school years, I identified seven things that became very significant in my life.

1. Career Change

When I was in grade twelve, the government announced that the new Number 1 Highway, the Trans-Canada Highway, would be routed across our farm and cut it in half. So, my dad sold both the south and the north pieces of our property. Now my father could go on to do what he had always wanted to do, become a building contractor. We moved to Clearbrook, bought six acres, subdivided the property, and began building homes for the growing population that was moving to the area. Dad also built some commercial buildings on South Fraser Way and other places in the greater Abbotsford area. I worked by his side during these years, and the skills he taught me were invaluable.

2. Athletics

I not only enjoyed athletics, but I had a passion for them. During my high school years, I participated in every athletic pursuit that was available. I especially enjoyed track meets. My best friend, Bruno, would always edge me out in the last few strides in the 100-yard dash. However, what I enjoyed most was pole vaulting. I joined the team to compete in an athletic competition at the high school in Lynden, Washington. Everything went well. I got first place and set a record for the track meet. Now all I had to do was stay healthy and do the same at our Mennonite Educational Institute in Abbotsford. However, as things happened, I tore the cartilage in my knee two days before the track meet. I tried to do some pole vaulting with a bandaged knee, but that only resulted in more pain. In fact, the pain was so intense that I started crying. I was brought to the hospital emergency room for treatment. Basically I was hearing God say to me, "What I want from you is not a track star, but a servant." I recommitted myself to serve Him in the time I was waiting for treatment for my knee.

3. Spiritual Commitment

During my teenage years, I had made a number of recommitments to follow the Lord completely. However, I always found myself falling back again and not following through as I had intended. A vivid picture that comes to mind is that I would find myself doing some work in a field with the tractor and suddenly be reminded of a sin that I had thought or committed. I would stop the tractor, get on my knees, and ask the Lord to be my Savior all over again. Some days I would recommit myself at least four times.

The study of 1 John, chapter 1 became significant in my understanding of what it meant to be a Christian. It was not my work, but God's work. It was not my holiness, but His holiness. 1 John 1:7 and 10 says, "If we walk in the light, as he is in the light...the blood of Jesus, his Son, purifies us from all sin. If we claim to be without sin, we deceive ourselves and the truth is not in us." I discovered that Christianity was made for imperfect people, tailor-made for imperfect people! That gave me hope, and a passion to tell others about this great salvation as well. I listened more carefully to sermons, read good books, and received good counsel from the numerous people whom I thought of as mature Christians. I was looking forward to serving the Lord in whatever way He wanted me to.

4. Friends

I had developed good friends. As a matter of fact, I found that the kind of friends I ran around with said a lot about who God was making me to be. We enjoyed ourselves, double dating, taking trips together, and spending Sunday afternoons at each other's homes.

When I was in grade twelve, my Dad helped me buy a '53 Chevy. I blanked it and had it painted candy apple red. Even I was surprised to see what it looked like when it came out of the shop. It was certainly an eye catcher.

Before grade thirteen classes began, some friends, Cliff and Jerry Hiebert and Rudy Thiessen, and I left for Seattle to buy clothes for the upcoming school year. We decided on the way that we would go to Los Angeles instead. So, we traveled day and night until we got there. We had more fun, told more stories, and shaped more stories than you can imagine. We had the whole muffler system in the car fall apart on one occasion. We stopped at a service station late at night, and the operator said he'd weld it up for us if we'd buy him a beer. I had never purchased something like that before. But we went ahead and bought him a beer, and he did the job for us. The car drove well all the rest of the trip.

Bruno Fast, a good friend of mine, was a houseguest in our home during the whole grade twelve year. He was a great influence on my life. As a high school teacher several years later, he died of an aneurism. We all miss him dearly. Friends are significant. Friends shape our future.

5. Carol

Dating was a great part of my high school experience. I'll always remember the time when my good friend, Bruno Fast, pointed out a beautiful, blonde-haired, blue-eyed girl in school who was a year or two younger than us. According to Bruno, she would become a very beautiful young lady. I looked, and I found myself agreeing with him.

There was a tradition of each boy choosing a girl to help serve with him at the Christmas banquet. I beat out my friend in asking Carol to do that with me. I was quite excited to have her at my side. Several weeks later, there was a skating event at Lysaaks' pond. I asked Carol if she'd go with me, and, to my delight, she said yes. We enjoyed the skating—until she broke through a thin place on the ice. I had an excuse to put my arms around her and pull her out of the water. She said she was surprised that her parents did not get upset with me for taking her on a dangerous skating trip. But that was the beginning of a long-term dating relationship.

6. Ministry

Carol was a sincere Christian, and I respected her for that. I recall talking to her at the end of grade twelve in a sentence that sounded something like this: "Carol, I know that we've been dating for quite a while now, and before we go any further, I need to tell you that I'm planning on entering the ministry. If that isn't something that you would want to do, why don't you tell me about that now, because it will make all the difference in the decisions we have ahead of us." She didn't take very long to respond with a "Yes"—she would want to be at my side even if I was a minister. I was excited and thankful.

Carol and I both tried out our skill at ministry. We both joined a home missions team under the West Coast Children's Mission, a Mennonite Brethren outreach, to teach vacation Bible school (VBS) in two different areas. Carol taught with a friend of hers in the Hope/Princeton area, and I taught with my friend, Herb Voth, in the Point Roberts area of northwest Washington state near the ocean.

I recall going with him on a Sunday afternoon to all the homes we could find in the neighborhood and inviting the children to the Grange, where we would conduct VBS starting early Monday morning. I had never taught before; I had simply observed how others taught. We had about thirty to forty kids come out on Monday morning. Herb taught the older kids, and I taught the younger ones. I'm glad there weren't too many people observing me as I taught because I was doing something brand new. However, after two weeks, a number of kids had received the Lord. We enjoyed a good closing program, and someone came and told me that they could see a budding minister in me.

When I got home, I was invited to lead the VBS for our home church. Also, I began teaching young boys in Sunday school on the weekends. These were all initial tries at ministry. I thank God for people who were patient with me as I was trying to learn a new skill.

7. Great

Carol reminded me that one of my favorite expressions was "Wouldn't that be great!" My desire was to serve God. As I look back now on the years, I realize that God was giving me many opportunities to serve and shaping me in each and every situation. So, now we not only say, "Wouldn't it be great," but we also say, "It has been great."

But the best is yet to be.

Chapter 4
Completing MEI and Going to Bible College

"Wisdom is supreme; therefore get wisdom.
Though it cost all you have, get understanding."
Proverbs 4:7

One of the demands of grade thirteen was to write government exams. I failed two of them, math and chemistry, and had to rewrite them in the middle of summer. I worked hard at reviewing the material and came through with good grades the second time around. I was very grateful to the Lord for this gift to me.

I had planned to go to Mennonite Brethren Bible College (MBBC) in Winnipeg and take my first year of Bible college to see how things worked out. I worked hard in construction over the summer in order to save up enough money to make the trip to Winnipeg and also to pay the tuition. It was a very positive experience. Carol planned to stay back and take her grade thirteen at MEI, while I traveled to Winnipeg and began my courses there. We were committed to each other, but we knew that it would be a good test to be separated for a year or two to see how our relationship would work out then.

In the fall of 1960, Carol and several friends gathered at the train station in Mission, B.C., in order to see us off on our way to Winnipeg. The traveling group included Bruno Fast, Sig Polle, my future brother-in-law, and myself. There were more than a few tears shed as we said goodbye to each other. This was taking a leap of faith in following the Lord.

We had fun traveling. Sig Polle, the creative chef, had brought along a big loaf of bread, together with liver sausage. The aroma wafted through the railway car, and people were wishing they had what we were eating.

Meanwhile, outside the window was some of the most spectacular scenery I'd ever seen in my life. Way back in 1946, when I had traveled with Mom and my siblings to British Columbia, I hadn't been aware of the beauty of this route. The thought occurred to me that there are new things one sees at different stages of life. Right now, I saw a great opportunity to study and prepare to serve the Lord. Of course, I would need His help all the way and His grace for each day's work.

When we arrived in Winnipeg, I met Henry Heidebrecht, my Dad's first cousin. He had a family of about six kids and was a very lively person. He took me around Winnipeg and introduced me to various places that I wanted to see. By trade, he was a painter, and he offered me a job painting part time with him if I so desired.

When I got to the Bible college, I was put up in a residence called "The White House." MBBC was the elite ministry school for Mennonite Brethren in Canada. There were students from every province from Ontario to British Columbia. It was exciting to get to know the other students and discover their backgrounds. I'll never forget that when I arrived there the first evening, there were a group of fellows playing touch football. I joined in. It was enjoyable to start off with a football game rather than with classroom studies.

When it came to the day for registration, I had to admit I didn't know many of the teachers except for F.L. Peters, so I asked the registrar for counsel on the best courses they had that would lead to ministry. I ended up with David A. Ewert for exegetical studies,

J. Toews for homiletics and sociology, J.A. Toews for history and Mennonite studies, and F.C. Peters for psychology and the Gospels. It was a very rich time as I sat at the feet of these great scholars and listened to them talk about the course material, their convictions, and the implications for our lives.

The first two years I studied all the basic subjects and also took some university courses that were accredited through Waterloo Lutheran University in Waterloo, Ontario. Between classes, we enjoyed the ping pong room, which was a place of intense athleticism, a great relief from the tension of studies. There was a gym next door, where we played basketball. We had great fun getting used to dorm life, playing jokes on one another, and living in community.

During that first year, I entered the speech contest and won second prize for a speech on the danger of nuclear war. In the second year, I was nominated as a candidate for president of the student body. So was my good friend, Henry Schmidt. He was elected—and deservedly so. I served as vice president. Interestingly, many years later at seminary in Fresno, I would be elected president of the student body, and he would be vice president. So, things have a way of evening out.

Making Plans

After Carol finished grade thirteen, she went on to a different Bible college, Bethany Bible Institute in Hepburn, Saskatchewan. So, we both had a chance to upgrade our Bible skills and ministry insights. Carol and I wrote letters to one another almost daily. Today we have a shoe box of letters that have gone unread since the time that we spent separated from one another during my first two years of college.

Carol and I had always talked about getting married after I had finished university. However, as we reflected on our future, more and more we felt that we might want to get married earlier than that. So that was left on the back burner. During my second year of Bible college, I turned twenty-one in February. During spring break, I drove up to Hepburn to visit with Carol. I had suggested to her that we reconsider our plans for when we would get married. So, taking her for a ride on a muddy road out in the country, I surprised her by asking her to marry me. She was delighted to say, "Yes." There, we stood and embraced each other and promised ourselves to each other in marriage. We came to the conclusion that neither of us had enough money to make it through college by ourselves, so pooling our resources might even be better. Of course, love is blind—and we enjoyed our blindness! We had no debt, and we did have some money saved up, so we could see how God would lead us in that as well. We were certain then that the best was yet to be!

Chapter 5
Marriage and Other Wonderful Things

*"He who finds a wife finds what is good
and receives favor from the LORD."*
Proverbs 18:22

When I came home from Bible college that spring, I bought an engagement ring. One evening, I talked to Carol's parents, asking for the privilege of having Carol's hand in marriage. I began talking to Mr. Ewert, but as soon as he realized what I was going to be talking about, he slowed me down and called for Mrs. Ewert to come and join us. I explained that I was in love with their daughter and was looking forward to marrying her. They approved and asked me about the timing. They were very encouraging of our relationship. Then Mr. Ewert gave me some warnings about things I should watch for when thinking about marrying Carol—she had good taste but that sometimes cost money, she was a strong person, etc. These were all things that I was aware of and appreciated in her.

Later that same week, I took Carol for a ride in my "new" 1952 Pontiac to Cultus Lake. We stopped at Maple Bay and went for a walk along the shore of the lake. There, on a cedar log, I opened a box and presented the engagement ring to her. Even though we had talked about it and had planned on getting engaged, it was still a thrill for both of us when the question was asked and she said, "Yes, I want to marry you." I have never been happier in my whole life. We drove home and announced the decision to her parents. Then I went to my home, burst into the living room, and told my parents. Everyone was very happy for the decision and encouraged us.

Now we had preparations to make for the wedding. There were the invitations, the flowers, the dresses, and all those other details that are part of the grand experience. It was a wonderful summer. Carol and I went for many drives where we held hands, embraced, and let our eyes sparkle with the anticipation of getting married. We had looked forward to this for years, and now it was about to become a reality. I recall that on one occasion when we drove to Chilliwack, I said, "I think the Lord will return before we get married. I can't imagine being so privileged as to be married to you and to enjoy a life together." The Lord didn't return, we were married, and it was an unforgettable experience.

We had been engaged on June 5, 1962. Our marriage would take place on September 7. When that great day arrived, the nuptials took place at the Clearbrook Mennonite Brethren Church. It was a church of young couples at that time, and the building was big enough for a large crowd. We had two ministers serve us, William Neufeld and Carol's pastor, H.H. Nickel. In that day, it was customary for the groom to usher the bride down the center aisle; when we got to the front, there were two chairs tied together with ribbons where the couple would be seated during the service. I was glad I could sit and relax and listen to the sermon, rather than standing and being nervous. After that, both of us had to pray an audible prayer of worship and thanksgiving. I listened to those prayers on tape later, and it did sound as if I was just a little nervous—but it was a good kind of nervous!

After the ceremony, we had a great celebration in the church basement. Sixteen men from our years at MEI presented several numbers in song. When everything was finally cleared up from the wedding ceremony, Carol and I left for Chilliwack for the first night of our honeymoon. We got to the Green Gables Motel on the east side of Chilliwack, unpacked our suitcases, and got ready for the first night. We were just doing our devotions, when I heard a hissing sound outside our motel. Later on, I found out that my sister, Rosa, had checked my wallet and found a receipt indicating where we were going to stay the first night. As a result, she and some other friends showed up outside our honeymoon suite. My, what a racket they made!

We didn't spend all the nights of our honeymoon in motels because we didn't think we had enough money. The next night, we went up to Nicola Lake and enjoyed being like Abraham for about four days, living in tents. Carol was the only one who caught a fish when we tried our skill at casting hooks into the lake. Next, we went through Vernon and Penticton and other cities in the interior of B.C. It was a good time.

My parents celebrated their twenty-fifth anniversary two weeks after our wedding. I recall that as emcee I grandly announced that, as a result of having "much experience in marriage," I had some advice for Mom and Dad. It brought a few laughs! I was really grateful for all the love and encouragement Mom and Dad had given Carol and me. They really wanted us to succeed and were pleased that we were serving the Lord.

Then, we packed what we could into our '52 Pontiac and drove off towards Winnipeg. I remember Carol falling asleep on my shoulder as I sang every song that I could think of to help her feel comforted about leaving home. We stopped at a motel in Saskatchewan, which was not exactly a five-star hotel, and went to some greasy spoon to pick up some food—and all of a sudden she was crying. I thought that I was surely a failure as a husband since I had not been able to stop this kind of passionate outpouring. I soon discovered that tears are not unusual in relationships.

Married Students

We arrived safely in Winnipeg and rented a suite in the Ebenezer apartment block, which was connected to Mennonite Brethren Bible College. This was an odd apartment block, with limited storage space for food and other necessities. Each suite was basically one room with a curtain between the sleeping area and the eating area. So, if you fried onions in the kitchen, you'd certainly smell it in the bedroom. There was also limited provision for normal activities such as taking a shower. There was one shower on the whole floor of apartments. The single students got a buzz out of watching the newly married couples go and use the shower together. We also had some wonderful water fights on that floor. It was a good year of study, relaxation, and celebration.

Students at the Bible college developed their speaking skills by preaching in towns such as Domain and Niverville on Sunday nights. The weather was often extremely cold, and the car tires would become rigid, with a flat side on the bottom. It took half a block of driving until the tires regained their circular shape and rolled smoothly again. I was encouraged by the response that we received from our preaching ministry that year. Abe Klassen and I took turns doing the honours in the various churches we attended. Our wives, Carol and Alvina, faithfully accompanied us.

I also had numerous opportunities to preach in my home church in Clearbrook when I was home during the summer months. This was good preparation for a preaching ministry. My father would be listening with tears flowing down his cheeks as he heard his son declare God's Word. He was deeply moved by the calling that God had placed on my life. Mom had a similar experience listening to me. She especially affirmed the freedom I had to tell stories and relax the audience as I spoke.

Looking Ahead

As I neared the end of my college studies, I let my name stand with J.J. Toews, our homiletics teacher, indicating that Carol and I were available to candidate if a church would choose to contact us. I'll never forget the note Dr. Toews left for me to come to his office the next Monday morning because there was a church interested in me pastoring their congregation. It was very exciting but scary at the same time. Would I be able to handle the interview? And would I be able to do the job of pastoring? The thing that affirmed me the most was the fact that I had a great sense of calling to go in the direction I was heading.

But the best was yet to be!

Chapter 6
The North Dakota Years

"Don't let anyone look down on you because you are young,
but set an example for the believers in speech, in life, in love,
in faith and in purity."
1 Timothy 4:12

I could hardly wait for Monday when I could go to Dr. Toews's office and find out more about the church that was inquiring about a pastor. The first thing I discovered was that the church was not in Canada but rather in the United States. The professor shared openly about my suitability for such a call. The church had about eighty members and was in the village of Sawyer in the rich agricultural area of North Dakota.

It was an exciting time as we thought about our first call to ministry. We knew nothing about Sawyer, North Dakota, and had no knowledge of the people there prior to our call. I talked with my professors, and they seemed to be positive about us taking this step and checking out the church. I received the same response from my fellow students.

Sawyer did have a history of having new Bible college graduates come and have their first pastoral experience in this small community. So we responded with a phone call to Sawyer saying that we would be available to come and candidate. We made arrangements to go there in two weeks. The candidating process really can be a Protestant purgatory at times. But we thought we would give it a shot. We prayed a lot, did some dreaming, and asked our friends to support us in prayer so that we would make a good decision.

The Candidating Process

It was late March when Carol and I made our trip to Sawyer, which was about eighty miles from Winnipeg. We crossed the border at the Peace Garden crossing and made our way down to Sawyer. There still was snow at the side of the road, and there was a brisk wind in the air. But we hardly noticed, we were so exciting about facing our first major test in ministry. Carol had been working the last winter at the Royal Bank of Canada, and she was tired and a little anxious about the weekend. She fell asleep in the front seat of the car and looked very peaceful. Carol was sleeping, and I was driving. I spent time with the Lord, trying to think through the issues that were before us as a couple.

Albert Beck was the church moderator. When we arrived at Albert and Martha's place, they had dinner ready for us, and we enjoyed an excellent meal with them. He was anxious to give us a lot of information about the church so we could be apprised of some of the needs and desires the church had. The Becks had done this before. Here I was, twenty-two years old, and Carol barely twenty, and we were testing out our ministry skills with people around us who were in their sixties. It seemed kind of odd.

After dinner and before it got dark, the Becks took us into town to see where the church was and also to see some of the sights of the area. Of course, we were anxious to see the lay of the land. Albert did a good job of selling the town—he was also the mayor. Sawyer was a town of about three hundred people. There was a general store, a restaurant, a post office, and a service station by the highway, which was selling petrol for sixteen cents a gallon—what a change the years have brought! Carol was especially excited to see that the parsonage was white, two stories in height, with a white picket fence around it. She had read a romance novel which had talked about a minister coming to town and moving into a parsonage which was similar in decoration. She liked the book, and she liked the town as well. She was positive about things before we started looking at the details.

We also met Wes and Mavis Vix, who were good, supportive members of the church. On Friday, they took us to Minot to see the big city of the area. Minot was a military center with air force installations and a population of around 40,000. We enjoyed getting a peek at the community and also having dinner at a local restaurant. We ordered some Italian food, and the waiter put a bib around me to protect me from splashes. I resisted, but he told me that everybody wore this bib if they wanted to have Italian food. I guess I thought that putting a bib around my neck would indicate how young I really was—and I wasn't eager to do that. I was pretty insecure as a pastoral candidate.

On Sunday morning, there was a light snow and a brisk wind. The joke they told me was that on any given day real estate was transferred from one farm to another without the assistance of a real estate agency. It just blew from one location to another, and there was no stopping it.

I had gone to the T. Eaton Company in Winnipeg to buy a hat to make myself look a little older than I really was. One parishioner asked me, "Do you always wear a hat?" I fibbed and said, "Most often." The truth is, this was the first time I had ever worn a formal hat. It was not a very good start for a man committed to preaching God's truth.

The former pastor, A.L. Klassen, led the service. I did not know that his son, who was two years old at the time, would one day be a fellow pastor with me at Northview Community Church in Abbotsford. God has interesting ways of connecting us with one other.

On Sunday morning, I preached a message which I had used in my home church at a prior time. I was rather nervous and felt awkward about preaching to a group of people who were examining me as a potential pastor. I spoke formally, and I was insecure about how I had delivered the message. After a relaxing afternoon, I came back to speak at the evening service. In that message, I decided to speak without notes and share my heart for ministry and the Lord. By God's grace, it went much better. Later, when the church made a decision regarding our candidacy, I was told that it was the evening service that had won them over to call us. The Lord was good and helped us in our weakness.

Before we left Albert Beck's place late that Sunday night, he filled my car with gas from his barnyard pump. He told us that the church would make a decision regarding our candidacy by Wednesday of that week. It seemed like a long time until that day came. On the way home, we had a good conversation about what it would look like to pastor a church like this. We were anxious to see what the church had decided. One moment we were glad that we had gone there to candidate, and the next moment we were anxious about how the whole thing would turn out. But the day came, and the church called us to come and be their pastor. Hallelujah!

The Central District Conference of Mennonite Brethren Churches in the United States had a long tradition of hiring young Canadian pastors to come and fill their pulpits. One of my good friends, Edmund Janzen, had come down to North Dakota the previous year and was pastoring in Harvey, North Dakota. We were looking forward to strengthening our friendship with him and his wife, Mary, and learning from one another how to pastor in this new country with different traditions than we were used to. Henry and Elvira Schmidt, who were pastoring in Oneida, South Dakota, were also dear friends and made our stay in Sawyer exciting as we visited with each other quite often.

Getting Started

When school was over, I sent Carol back to British Columbia by train so she could spend some time with her parents and friends and organize our stuff that needed to be packed and brought to North Dakota. Meanwhile, I would get things set up in Sawyer. Art Vix, another wonderful church member, came with his pickup truck to transport our possessions from Winnipeg to Sawyer. He smiled and laughed when he saw that we only had about half a pickup load of goods to bring down to our new home in North Dakota. He assured me that after a few years we would be able to fill a large truck with our furnishings. "That's just the way it is," he said. He was right!

I enjoyed the conversation I had with Art. He had a great sense of humor and was upbeat and fun to drive with. He talked non-stop all the way back to Sawyer, and when he wasn't talking, he was singing. He had a little ditty in his mind that he sang over and over again: "Does your chewing gum lose its flavor on the bedpost overnight?" I decided this would be an interesting church. It's amazing the things one remembers about meeting a new friend.

I had sold my '52 Pontiac before I came down with Art Vix to Sawyer so we wouldn't have the hassle of bringing it into the United States. When I got there, I went with one of the elders to a local car sales place to buy a car. They convinced me to buy a new car so we'd have good transportation in the snowy winter and the dusty summer. After examining the various car lots, I picked up a 1963 Chevy. A local farmer, a church member, financed it for me. It was a perk that I hadn't expected.

Since I was not a citizen of the United States and had no financial record of doing business there, I had to drive down to Bismarck, the capital of North Dakota, to get the vehicle registration. It was good to have another church member with me to enjoy the trip, and the guidance I received from him was helpful as well.

I had a good sleep and then drove all the way to British Columbia to see Carol and her family and mine. Our parents had lots of questions about the pastoring we would do and our plans for the future. After a few days, we packed the new car with the things that we had left with our parents and drove east to North Dakota. Everything went well except for one night in Montana when we went into a motel to check out the price. Upon returning to our car, we discovered we had been robbed. Carol's wedding pearls and many other goods that we had received as gifts had disappeared. That's just the way it goes sometimes. But we did make it safely to Sawyer. We were anxious to get started.

We arrived in Sawyer Friday morning. The parsonage was "spick and span" clean, and the shelves were filled with groceries. What a great welcome for a new pastoral couple!

We had been informed that there would not be a normal morning service that first Sunday. Val Cloud, a traveling evangelist, had set up his tent across the street from the church, and our congregation, together with several other congregations, would enjoy worship together in this tent. So we both slept in a bit on Sunday morning. I got up earlier than Carol, put on my suit jacket, and walked to the church, which was only a block away. To my surprise, the whole congregation was sitting there waiting for their pastor to come and speak to them. I checked with an elder and asked what was going on. "We're having a welcoming service for you prior to the Val Cloud meeting," he said. Somehow we had got the dates and times mixed up.

I excused myself and ran to the parsonage as fast as I could. Fortunately, Carol was almost dressed and ready to go. We huffed and puffed our way into the church. On the way, I mentioned to her that the congregation were looking forward to each of us giving a talk about our feelings concerning the new assignment that we had accepted. We hadn't finalized what we were going to say, but we adlibbed. We both talked, but I can't remember what we said. I only know that I was nervous and Carol cried. I was informed that Carol's message came across more powerfully than mine. What a start! However, I did say a few words at the Val Cloud revival session, and they were well received. So now we had made a start in ministry. I observed that to be a minister would require readiness at all times.

Learning on the Job

We were fortunate indeed that the church members were very loving, supportive, and helpful in our ministry. They welcomed us and treated us as people fully equipped for ministry. Another thing which struck me was that everyone called me "Reverend" or "Pastor." I wasn't used to having that kind of title attached to my name. It took a while to get used to it, but it came with time. The word got around town that the Sawyer Mennonite Brethren Church had a pastor with a teenage wife. It was not quite true—Carol was twenty years old.

When I went to North Dakota, I was still short two courses to complete my Bachelor of Theology degree from Mennonite Brethren Bible College. Fortunately, Minot State University was only a thirty-minute drive away. With the church's permission, I was able to take those two courses at the university the next year and to complete enough other courses over the next two years to give me a Bachelor of Arts degree, with a major in American history and a minor in the German language. It was good to be able to study on this secular university campus and then bring back new insights to the church.

It was interesting how I experienced some of the firsts in ministry during my time in Sawyer. The first counseling session I had was on the initial day of sitting in my office. A deacon came in and asked me to give him a biblical reason why he could not marry a divorcee and continue on as a deacon. The church was against it, and he asked me to help him work through making this potential marriage a reality. I sat behind the desk feeling pretty small. The question was difficult, and was laced with politics of the town. I hadn't taken a course in Bible college on how to deal with that situation. So I took a little while to work that issue through.

The first funeral at which I officiated was also noteworthy. The gentleman who had passed away was already a friend of ours. He had loaned us his speedboat for waterskiing and fishing and enjoying the Lake District in North Dakota. The church was filled to capacity, and I went down into the basement to arrange things with the family before we all walked up to participate in the funeral service. There I found members of the family arguing with each other about who would receive what in the inheritance. This was again an issue that took months to work through. I was beginning to feel that I didn't belong in the ministry, with so many intricate and politically charged situations to deal with. One thing I learned about the ministry was that I should never be surprised about anything. Surprises were always around the corner.

Then there was the first wedding. I was excited to prepare this couple for marriage. As a bold young minister, I asked them in premarital counseling whether or not they had been intimate with each other. They assured me they had lived a life that didn't include that dynamic. Yet, within six months after the wedding, she had a baby. Short pregnancy, I guess. When I questioned them about this, their simple response was, "We didn't want you to stop our plans for a church wedding." I was disappointed! It didn't take long to discover that many people had great expectations of the pastor to be able to negotiate with people through difficult situations.

Expectations of the church were not too high. The basic job description in the church was to preach Sunday morning and Sunday night and also lead the Wednesday night prayer meeting and Bible study. Beyond that, they wanted me to visit every home at least twice a year. This aspect of the ministry I truly enjoyed because it endeared us to the people. There's something special that happens when you visit people in their homes and talk about life and pain and exciting new developments. I had a chance to hear people up close and personal, pray with them, and encourage them.

Another thing I discovered was that agrarian people also liked it when I got up close and personal with the jobs on their farms. In my spare time, I was invited to do some renovations for individuals who had small jobs to be taken care of. Since I had learned quite a few carpentry skills from my father, I added a room to one house, put new ceilings in some houses, and laid flooring in others. In the fall, when the combines harvested grain, I packed it away in bins for later trucking to the city. I especially enjoyed working for Harry Sylstead. He didn't attend the Sawyer church, but he owned a large farm and appreciated the services that I gave him in terms of farm work. I cultivated hundreds of acres of property for him, sowed grain, swathed grain, and hauled grain to the elevator.

When doing these jobs, I always had my farm Bible on the seat next to me in the truck. I found that I could read through the Bible at least twice a year during the off times when I was waiting for the combine to unload grain into the truck, and then for the grain to be unloaded from the truck into the grain bins. It made the day go by quickly, and it was very enriching, as I was able to learn a lot as a young minister concerning the Scriptures.

Sometimes I didn't dress appropriately because I was a British Columbia boy unused to prairie winters. One afternoon, I left to do some house visitation, wearing just a light jacket. As I entered the countryside, I realized there was snow piled up, with some drifts crossing the road, and the weather had turned considerably colder. I was nearly at the home that I was going to visit, and I noted that there was a snowdrift across the road just prior to the farmer's driveway. My thinking went something like this, "If I don't make it through the snowdrift, I can always get the farmer to pull me out of the drift with his tractor." I gunned the motor and tried to make it through the drift but failed miserably. I went to the door of the church member, but he wasn't home. I decided to walk to another member's home, which was about a mile and a half down the road to the east. I managed to walk there, but to my dismay there was no one home there either. Then it dawned on me. It was John Deere day in town, when everybody went in to look at the new equipment. So I had to walk back the same distance I had walked before. The wind was getting colder, and my limbs were starting to shiver. I made it back to the place where my car was hung up on the drift and decided to head further west towards the farm of Mr. and Mrs. Kline. This was another three miles. By now, the wind was turning biting cold. The sun was down, and the cold was severe. Halfway walking towards the farmhouse I was looking for, I could hardly put one foot in front of the other. I began to wonder if someone would find me on the road half frozen. But, by God's grace, I hung in and walked all the way to the Klines' home. Fortunately, they had returned from John Deere day by then. I banged on the door, and they opened it. I stumbled in and was unable to talk. My face was frozen. The Klines were kind enough to thaw me out slowly and then drive me home. Our church member pulled my car off the road and into his yard, and I picked the automobile up the next day. That was one of the hazards of house visitation on a cold day.

Expanding Horizons

God has unique ways of expanding our horizons. I became a traveling evangelist for a while as part of my experience. A church in Johns Lake, North Dakota, invited me to come and lead a series of evangelistic meetings. I agreed. The church made posters and put them up in all the highly visible places in the town. The weekend the evangelistic meetings began, I went with the pastor to visit the homes of people who were not interested in Christianity and try to convince then to come to the sessions that we were having. There was also a telephone campaign to invite people to be present. I preached my heart out. I was surprised that there were people who made recommitments to the Lord and even some who were born again.

Word got out that I was an evangelist. So, I found myself doing this kind of preaching in Frazer, Montana; Delft, Montana; Oneida, South Dakota; and several other places. I made it a practice to drive home the night after the last meeting. It was always a delight to see Carol after a week of preaching.

After several years of ministering in Sawyer, the church decided they wanted to ordain me for the ministry. This was an exacting event where my theology was checked out, my ministry and lifestyle were examined, and the evidence of God's call on my life was reviewed. Carol's parents and my parents came down from Canada for this special event. We had a great deal of fun as a family, especially because it included showing off our first son, Murray, who was six months old. Grandfather Heidebrecht was extremely proud of him.

These were busy years. We were pastoring the church and were also leading the youth ministry. Along with this, we were responsible for maintaining the facilities, which meant mowing the lawn in the summer and shoveling snow in the winter.

Carol was kept busy with the birth of two more boys. After Murray, Bobby and Davy joined our family.

In February of 1968, I took a trip to Palestine. I had found a tour company that made a free trip available to a pastor if the pastor had a large enough group to accompany him on the trip. I'll never forget the first time I woke up in old Jerusalem, looking out the window and experiencing the noises and sights just as they would have been during the time of Jesus. We enjoyed touring through Palestine and visiting the old sites, some of which seemed to have been changed considerably for commercial reasons. We were also aware of the Six-Day War that had just taken place. Military equipment stood abandoned beside the road in quite a few places. Besides Israel, we also stopped in Greece, Rome, and London. Carol took our sons, Murray and Bob, with her to British Columbia while I made this trip. She did have two opportunities to accompany me on similar trips to Israel later on in our life.

Those were exciting opportunities, but the best was yet to be.

Chapter 7
California, Here We Come

"The path of the righteous is like the first gleam of dawn,
shining ever brighter till the full light of day."
Proverbs 4:18

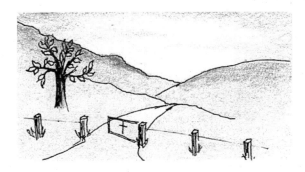

Carol and I had prayed much and reflected on whether we should go to Mennonite Brethren Biblical Seminary in Fresno, California. We became convinced it was a logical next step for us, and we were prepared to invest the time and the finances to do this. However, we were not able to see how we could do this on our own. So, we gave ourselves to prayer regarding the financing of this segment of our lives.

There was a man named Walt Neumann who lived south of town. His house burned down, and he shared with me that God had given him a vision that I would be rebuilding his home for him. I received approval from the church leadership to do that. The community was aware that the pastor was building a house, so I often had visitors come by to watch—and also to help! The money I received for this work enabled us to go to seminary.

The church had a wonderful farewell party for us. We found it hard to hold back tears as we said goodbye to a group of people who meant so much to us. There's something about the first ministry experience and the connecting that goes on there that is distinctive.

But the greatest gift during those five years in Sawyer was the three sons that the Lord gave us. Murray James, born November 21, 1964, was a handsome young man with a lot of charisma. Robert Lorne, born May 31, 1966, was a wonderful addition to Murray. They enjoyed playing together, and Murray was an older brother and model for his younger sibling. David Lynn, born July 7, 1968, made the trip with us to California when he was just three weeks old. Karla Marie was born October 24, 1970, some years later, in San Jose, California.

That summer of 1968, we had a safe, 1,300-mile trip to Fresno, California, with only two forced stops, one for a flat tire and the second for adjusting the furniture in the trailer so that we could have a smoother ride. What surprised us the most, when we came from the mountains down into the San Joaquin Valley, was how hot it was, over 100 degrees Fahrenheit. It was something we would have to get used to. A good friend, Elmo Warkentin, along with his wife, Sarah, put us up in his home for the first few days. Elmo was the director of education and evangelism for the US Mennonite Brethren Conference. He did everything he could for us to have a smooth transition to seminary life. We found a rental home within walking distance of the seminary and Butler Avenue Mennonite Brethren Church.

We had received a call to serve as the associate pastor couple of this church in Fresno. The church had not had a person on staff in this position before, so they sent a job description my way, and I tailored it to what I thought I could do. That would be limited, as I was going to attempt to do a three-year seminary degree in only two years. Still, the workload was pretty heavy. I was responsible for the high school youth ministry, the university student ministry (we were a campus church for Fresno Pacific College), emceeing the morning and evening services, preaching at least once a month, and helping to recruit Sunday school teachers for the education department—all for a salary of $250 a month. We were grateful for the invitation. Busy as it was, we were up for the challenge, with many supportive team members helping us. Another unique dynamic of this church was that it was the home church for many of the professors of the seminary and also the college. It was a challenge to minister to the needs of these educated folks, but, by God's grace, it went well.

Divine Innovation

So, we started seminary. In the spring of the first year, I was taking an evangelism class which included a field trip to the San Francisco Bay area to see the new, innovative things that were happening in the churches there. I was most impressed with the ministry of Dr. Ray Stedman at Peninsula Bible Church in Palo Alto, California. Later, I would write my master's dissertation on his church.

Returning from this field trip, we stopped at Lincoln Glen Church in San Jose, which was a large Mennonite Brethren congregation. When I looked at the church, I said to my classmates that this was the kind of place where I would never want to come and minister since it was too traditional. I had hopes of planting a church in Kamloops, British Columbia, not San Jose, California. The Lord has a way of showing us His sense of humor. Later that summer, Carol and I received a call from the Lincoln Glen Church to fill the pulpit for the weekend. We gladly accepted the call, and were looking forward to the preaching assignment. Harry and Rubena Baerg were our hosts for the weekend. About halfway through Saturday of that weekend, Harry broached the subject of me candidating as a pastor in Lincoln Glen. I assured him that that was not our intention and we hadn't given much thought to that kind of assignment. However, Harry assured me that the church was expecting to see a pastoral candidate that weekend. I asked if I could use his office to rework some of my message for the occasion.

The next morning, when we were getting ready to go to church, I took my jacket off the hanger, only to discover to my dismay that I had left my pants in Fresno. A pastoral candidate with only a jacket and no pants would not be very appropriate. We didn't know what to do. So, I asked Harry if he had an extra suit that I could wear for the occasion. He said, "Yes, I do." I tried it on, and it was pretty snug—and a luminous bright green. This would be a winner for sure. I preached in that suit and must have kept people awake with my brightly colored attire.

We returned to seminary life and, with much prayer, allowed our name to stand as a pastoral candidate. The church cast a ballot, and it was overwhelmingly in favor of us coming. I told the church that it would be a year before we could come to pastor because I was in seminary full time. However, the church suggested we try living in two homes—the church had a parsonage for us in San Jose for weekends, and we could keep our rental home in Fresno. It made sense. So, we had a year of traveling back and forth every weekend from Fresno to San Jose—a mere eighty-six miles one way. After spending Sunday evening preaching and visiting, we would get home at about one in the morning. On the trip back, our children would be sleeping, and Carol would be relaxing; that was a good time for me to catch up on my thinking as I drove.

A Stronger Call to Ministry

In the fall of that year, J.B. Toews, president of the seminary, invited Larry Martens and me to attend an evangelism conference in Minnesota led by Billy Graham. Dr. Toews's idea was to mentor us in preaching. He tried to arrange it so that every evening we would get a chance to preach in a different setting. It was a good learning experience. I recall especially one session when his evaluation of me included the admonition that I should say less often the phrase "It seems to me." He thought I should have a stronger call to ministry and a stronger vision.

One night on this trip, I stayed in the parsonage of the host pastor. I was having my evening prayer when I noticed that outside there was a full moon in a beautiful star-lit sky. I was attracted to the beauty of God and nature, and I sensed the Holy Spirit drawing me out of my room and into the adjacent field of twelve-foot high corn stalks. I got on my knees and asked the Lord to give me insight for both the large assignment I had at San Jose and my studies at the seminary. I had spent a good deal of time on my knees in the field when I began to get the distinct impression that the Lord was speaking to me. What I heard Him say is that He was calling me to develop churches with mission assignments that would encompass the whole world. I never forgot that call, and every church that I have served as a pastor has moved into a mission mindset. This was of God.

After arriving back home from this circuit of preaching and evaluation, I put my mind to work in writing my dissertation for seminary. The title was, "The Mission of the Church as Expressed in Its Biblical Images." Ray Stedman of the Peninsula Bible Church would be my mentor in preparing this dissertation. I spent a number of weekends in San Jose while my family was in Fresno. This gave me the time to research, test, and write my dissertation. I praise the Lord that it was done in time for graduation.

Again my parents came down for a graduation, and they were very affirming of what God was doing in our lives. That last year of seminary, we made that eighty-six-mile trip every weekend, and Carol and our three boys had to live out of two homes. Carol not only had three sons to take care of but was also expecting again. She was a trooper. I still don't know how we did it. It was definitely an adventure for our young family! We made it through that year and by God's grace moved to San Jose to start a new chapter of ministry. But really, the best was yet to be.

Chapter 8
The Way to San Jose

"My grace is sufficient for you, for my power is made perfect in weakness."
2 Corinthians 12:9

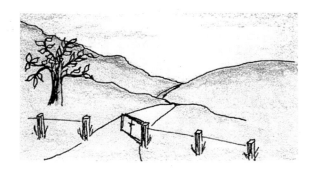

We completed our first year of ministry at San Jose while we were still completing seminary training in Fresno. It seemed like a dream! A busy section of our life was over, and now we anticipated putting our roots down deeper in San Jose and pastoring the Lincoln Glen Church .

When offering leadership training, I often present the following model: In his first year at a church, a pastor needs to enjoy the honeymoon; in the second year, he needs to discover the real issues of the church; in the third year, he needs to begin dealing with those issues or sidestepping them; and in the fourth year, he needs to either do the job or leave! Now I was about to see how I would fare in my second year at San Jose.

A Team of Friends

One of the first things I sought to do when I began the ministry in San Jose was to develop a discipleship team, a group of friends who would work together with me. One of the first people who showed himself to be a true friend was Harold Schroeder. He was the former associate pastor. The church had gone through some difficulties, and he said something like this to me, "I'm going to do everything I can to help you be successful. If there's any blame for mistakes, lay it on me. I want you to do well, Vern." He was truly a friend. Unfortunately, about fifteen years later, he died of cancer.

A new couple who began coming to our church about the time we began our ministry there was Ken and Dee Panbecker, who came to the church with their three sons. After several months of church attendance, Ken took me aside and said, "I really enjoy the way you lead the church. I don't think I've ever seen anyone who has the same skills in bringing the church together and setting out a vision." Whether this was all true or simply an encouragement, I can't say. But I do know that over the years Ken and Dee loved us, encouraged us, and said things to us that very few have ever said to us in the same way. They were real friends—and continue to be.

I prayed for a person I could disciple to work alongside me in developing an evangelistic team. God opened up the heart of Henry Boese to come alongside me and give his life to evangelism. Together, we went to an evangelism conference in Denver, Colorado, to brush up on our skills. Then we began building a visitation team. Every Tuesday night, our team went out and visited the homes of people who had connected with our church for the first time. If we had no contacts, we simply selected a section of the city and began visiting homes one by one. After the visitation was done, we would come back together for some dessert and coffee. It was exciting to see how many members of the team had found individuals who were looking for a church and other individuals who were looking for the Savior. There were many who came to the Lord during those days.

Another group of people got excited about a bus ministry. They bought a bus, developed a pattern of finding children who were interested in Sunday school, and then brought them to the church for the children's program. I wouldn't say this was the greatest success in terms of numbers, but it did give many individuals a chance to participate in evangelism.

The church had already been planning a building program when I was called to be the lead pastor. The church had purchased ten acres of property, and five acres had been used to build Lincoln Glen Manor, a senior citizens' development. After a series of business meetings, we decided to move out in faith and put the building that we were presently in, which was on Clark Street, on the market. My neighbor, Walter England, picked up the challenge to sell the building.

He was successful. We sold our building and had no place to worship—or so we thought. A congregation from the Church of God (Anderson, Indiana) denomination invited us to have our worship services in their building at 8:00 a.m. on Sunday mornings. They would then have their services at 9:30. Beyond that, we decided to have a joint Church of God/Mennonite Brethren service every Sunday night. The pastors took turns preaching, and it was delightful to get to know a whole different congregation in a worship setting. The highlight for me was when the Church of God people said, "Our services feel like a camp meeting." Obviously they had a history of lively camp meetings.

We built our new building using congregational skills. Members of the church worked on the building after their regular jobs were done for the day, during work bees, and on weekends. In 1972, the project was completed. It was exciting to move into something that was new and modern.

One thing we didn't have is multiple staff. We searched for a person to serve as minister of youth and education. God opened the door for a couple from Abbotsford, Ed and Carol Boschman, and their two girls to come and join us. The two and a half years that Ed and I spent together were phenomenal. We enjoyed working together, praying together, dreaming together, and strategizing together. Ed was a gifted musician and also a terrific leader. Later he would plant a church in Bakersfield, California, and then from that experience be called to lead the US Mennonite Brethren Conference as a full-time staff member.

Grace

One of the things that I personally had been dealing with over a number of years was the ability to speak publicly. Most of the time things worked well, but then there were days when I just was very nervous and insecure about communicating publicly. I had ministers lay hands on me and pray that the fear would leave me, but it just seemed to get worse. I recall a specific Sunday morning when I was in the study waiting for the choir to come so they could join me to go out onto the stage. I lay down on the floor in my study and said to the Lord, "It's not fair, Lord, that You are making this so difficult for me. You called me, and You asked me to be Your minister. Now I need help."

As I lay there on the floor, the words came to me from 2 Corinthians 12:9: "My grace is sufficient for you, for my power is made perfect in weakness." In that passage, Paul went on to say that he rejoiced in his weaknesses because when he was weak, then he was strong. The Lord gave me this insight: "Whenever you get nervous, just thank Me for it, as Paul thanked Me for his weakness in a previous century." So I joined the choir, and we went out onto the stage. As I stood behind the pulpit to begin speaking, again my heart started palpitating. I looked up and said, "Thank you, Lord. This is a gift from You." The result was that, within a few months, the anxiety had been dealt with. Consequently, this has become my Scripture verse for life: "My grace is sufficient for you, for my power is made perfect in weakness."

Carol's Testing

Carol also was tested in a very personal way. During a regular medical check-up in the doctor's office, a lump had been discovered in her breast. This caused anxiety in Carol because two of her sisters had struggled with cancer. We called together the elders and some friends, who anointed her with oil and prayed over her. I don't know if I ever felt so weak and needy as at that moment when we were praying over Carol. I broke down and cried while others tried to encourage Carol and me. We prayed for a miracle.

While we were waiting in the hospital for Carol's surgery, the doctor said to me, "If the surgery takes over an hour and fifteen minutes, it means I will be doing a mastectomy. If it takes less time than that, it should be clear."

So, I waited in the waiting room. After three hours of waiting, I was convinced that we were dealing with cancer. Just when I thought everything was over with Carol's health, the doctor walked in smiling and said that she had a clean bill of health.

I asked, "Why did it take so long?"

His response was interesting: "The tissue looked so much like cancer I had Carol stay under the anesthetic a longer time while I went across the street to the lab to do a double check on the tissue."

We looked at him and said, "It's a miracle." We had prayed. God had answered.

Family Blessing

The first great thing that happened to us in San Jose was the birth of our daughter, Karla Marie. It was a joy to have a girl in our home after having three wonderful boys. I'm not sure the boys always felt the same about the new addition.

The strain of the last few years—traveling back and forth a considerable distance for ministry, having four young children under foot, and keeping up with a demanding schedule—got to Carol. We made it a practice for years to have breakfast together every Monday morning and just sit and talk. It became a great occasion for us to get to know each other better and to develop intimacy—which made it easier to handle the tasks that were at hand.

Carol and I enjoyed going to anything where our children were involved. In the summer months, our boys played baseball. Murray was the big first baseman who slugged the home runs. Bob and Dave played infield, and both pitched as well. Karla played soccer. We never missed a game. For us, these events were as sacred as a church business meeting.

We are not exactly a musical family, but we did make a joyful noise to the Lord. Murray played the trumpet and banged away on the drums; Bob played the clarinet; Dave strummed the guitar; and Karla played the flute. It was very interesting to hear the music coming from our family. Carol insisted that everyone take a rudimentary course in piano playing in order to have a more balanced life.

Carol was into reading, and doing some kind of stitching at times. She enjoyed the reading especially. I enjoyed woodwork. A good friend of mine, Warren Karber, helped me develop a woodworking shop in my garage. With this beginning, I added a family room to the house and also built a set of cabinets and vanities for the various rooms in the home. I refinanced the house to take care of the added costs, but I saved considerable amounts because of the work I did myself.

From time to time, I hear people say they feel sorry for ministers' kids because they have all the "pastor types" staying at their home. "It must make for a lot of boring conversation," they suggest. Far from it. Where else could our children have heard exciting firsthand accounts of missionaries' adventures in deepest Africa, the highest Andes Mountains, or the Mexican countryside? Our kids had to give up their bedrooms from time to time when we had guests, ministers or missionaries, in our home. But this was also exciting because the missionaries would often give them a little token of appreciation. These were times of growth, filled with learning and adventure.

Traveling as a family was also exciting. At vacation time, we often packed the station wagon for the big trip to British Columba to see the children's grandparents, aunts, uncles, and cousins. This was a long, thousand-mile trek, and we brought along all kinds of learning devices to keep everyone interested on the way, including a reading library, games, and a stash of candies. We undertook these treks without seatbelts (which were not used in those prehistoric times), but, by God's grace, we never had an accident. Some years, we took an RV or tent trailer. Those were good family times. In the evenings, we enjoyed camping or staying at a motel which had a swimming pool. Along the way, the kids enjoyed guessing what kind of a welcome Grandpa and Grandma would give this year—verbally and materially. Would Grandma Ewert have her famous chicken noodle soup for us?

We built many treasured memories during our excursions to Canada. Then there were good times spent at Disneyland and the seaside town of Carpinteria. (On one of our beach adventures, I capsized the dinghy we were rowing. In a panic, the kids ran to inform Carol that I had lost my hairpiece. How exciting!) These were delightful years.

Our good friends, Ken and Dee, were planning on taking a trip to Europe. We visited with them and were convinced to join them on this adventure. So, in the summer of 1979, after bringing our four children to British Columbia to stay with the grandparents, aunts, and uncles, we took a one-month extended road trip through seven countries in Europe. This was exciting because we saw areas of the world we had not been exposed to before. We took side roads, stayed at bed and breakfasts, and visited the various historic places of Europe. It was a lot of fun and a refreshing period; it felt like a second honeymoon. We still have pictures, memories, and stories to tell from that once-in-a-lifetime trip.

Then there were surprises that came along that delighted the heart. Dale and Shirley Nachtigal owned a construction company. One day they said to one another, "If we make enough profit on our next building venture, we'll invite Vern and Carol to join us on a trip to Hawaii." What a delightful surprise! Friends generously took care of our four kids, and we enjoyed two weeks of fun in the sun.

Personal Growth

Personally, there were two things I was desiring in my own spiritual life. One was relational, and the second was intellectual.

Relationally, I wanted to discipline my life to be into the Word and to be inside the Spirit to a greater extent. I discovered a beautiful road south of San Jose that led right into the mountains. I drove there one Thursday and discovered a stream flowing near the road and a place where I could park my car and enjoy the scenery, the sounds, and the atmosphere. I spent some time praying there and decided to come back again the next week. Soon, this became a Thursday event for me. I would fast on Thursdays, read and memorize Scripture in the morning, and then write the first draft of my Sunday sermon on Thursday afternoon. Eventually, this led me into the whole concept of prayer journaling. This became a significant part of my life.

On the intellectual front, I enjoyed studying and started checking out the Bay area to see if there was a place where I could work on a doctorate. Golden Gate Baptist Theological Seminary in San Francisco appealed to me most. I liked that institution's theology, and it was only seventy-six miles from our home. I could do the work in one and a half days a week. But first I needed to pass three entrance exams: a Greek translation test, a Bible content test, and a graduate record exam. By God's grace, I passed all three. In a meeting, our congregation decided to approve my plans and support Carol and me in this adventure. In all the years that I have worked in church ministry, I have found churches to be very generous and helpful in making things possible which otherwise might not have been so. We were very grateful. After I graduated, a memory came to my mind of that high school teacher who had doubted whether I could graduate from high school with my grades. It was good to have a report card from the Seminary with straight A's. It was some kind of delight to see that God had helped me do something that looked impossible.

Restless

Meanwhile, God was giving me more opportunities for ministry all the time. I spoke at conventions and renewal meetings in Kitchener, Ontario; Hillsborough, Kansas; Tofield, Alberta; Corn, Oklahoma; Abbotsford, British Columbia (in both South Abbotsford and Central Heights Mennonite Brethren Churches); Willingdon Church in Burnaby, B.C.; Grand Forks, B.C.; and other places.

But, after spending eleven years in my first large church experience, I felt a restlessness. The church had undergone considerable change. It had become a more accurate reflection of the community it was in. Many missionaries had been sent out from the congregation into various parts of the world. Beyond that, leaders were being developed in the church. However, I felt I needed to start over again. I saw that some changes were needed in church administration and church leadership. I felt that it would be better for someone else to take the church to the next step of growth. I especially wished to work in a church that was open to having an eldership style of leadership. By this I mean that the elders would do actual ministry and not only administration. There were so many things that I felt I needed to improve on, and it seemed to me that God was calling me to leave San Jose and getting me ready to be planted elsewhere. As I know now, the best was yet to be.

IN THE BEGINNING

David and Katie Heidebrecht, with children Rosa, Agnes, George, Vern, and Ruth (inset)

A very young Vern

Build your barn before your house: The barn that Vern built as his dad's apprentice

HE WHO FINDS A WIFE FINDS WHAT IS GOOD

Vern   Wedding: September 7, 1962   Carol

Above all, get wisdom and understanding: Graduation from Golden Gate Baptist Theological Seminary in San Francisco, May 1977

CALLED TO MINISTRY

Sawyer: Our first pastorate, 1963

Visalia: First sermon

Coming home: Northview Community Church, Abbotsford, B.C., 1988

Northview: Community events were an opportunity to invite friends and neighbors

Northview: Building a gifted staff was critical

A JOY-FILLED FAMILY

Vern and Carol with their young family, on Esther Drive in San Jose, California

The children as teenagers and college students in Visalia, California

Murray and Holly with Noah and Avery

Bob and JoAnn with Karis, Connor, and Elisa

Dave and Michelle with Jonas, Jack, and Jase

Karla and Menno, October 10, 1998

Abbotsford: The last of four houses that Vern built

Maya, Karli, Brody, and Riley

Brothers and sisters: David and Ruth Sherk, Rosa Toews, mother Katie Heidebrecht, Dan and Agnes Ratzlaff, George and Kathy Heidebrecht, and Vern and Carol

FROM JERUSALEM TO THE ENDS OF THE EARTH

70th anniversary of a church in Tofield, Alberta, founded by Vern's grandfather

Preaching at the 70th anniversary

A taste of the Orient: Japan

In Russia with Garry Schmidt

From Paris with love

Receiving the Order of Abbotsford from Mayor George Ferguson

Chapter 9
Shaping an Urban Church

"A generous man will prosper;
he who refreshes others will himself be refreshed."
Proverbs 11:25

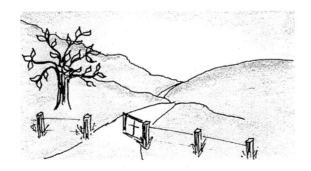

In 1980, after we received a call from Neighborhood Church in Visalia, California, I made a list of "talking points" which I would discuss with the church moderator, Bob Ewert. This was our first visit to Visalia, a pre-candidating meeting to lay out the parameters of our call before the Lord. On our way back with the information, Carol and I shared with each other and the children the possibility of moving to Visalia. We all agreed in principle that we would be open to the call.

When the call came and we made the decision to move to Visalia, we decided to look at the option of building a new house. It was a favorable time to sell a house in the Bay area and buy something in the San Joaquin Valley. For good measure, we decided to put in a swimming pool so our kids could enjoy the hot weather which is common in the valley. Moving with four children was an adventure.

We had more stuff than we realized. With two trucks, a car packed full, a cat, and lots of help, we made the move and began settling in.

Hearing God

The first Sunday in Visalia seemed odd. The sanctuary was about the size of the foyer in our former church in San Jose. With only 108 people in the first service and an even smaller group in the second, it almost felt like we were ministering to a small group rather than a whole congregation. But the church was warm, optimistic, and filled with faith. We looked forward to a new chapter in our life.

Early on in our ministry there, I asked the church to think of a place where I could meditate and study off campus. There was a lady in the church named Mary Barnett, who owned a cabin in the area known as Three Rivers, about thirty miles from Visalia. It was at the foot of the mountains in a beautiful spot overlooking the Kaweah River. She called it the "Prophets Cabin," and she generously offered to let me use it. For about seven years, I went to the Prophets Cabin once a week for study, sermon writing, and rest. This is where I got the basic idea for the book I wrote a number of years later, *Hearing God's Voice* (Cook Communications Ministries, 2007). This was a time of significant spiritual maturation for me, learning how to hear God's voice through reading the Scriptures, through observing nature, and through listening to what people were saying to me. Other ministers and writers also used the cabin for the same purpose.

Used by God

In the spring of 1982, I was invited to be the evangelistic speaker at a crusade in Abbotsford, British Columbia. The new gym at Mennonite Educational Institute had just been completed, and the organizers wanted to use the facilities for this event. Seventeen churches got together and prepared for an evangelistic thrust into the community. They asked me to speak at the main event, and Ed Boschman to speak at MEI student body gatherings.

This was a real test of faith on my part, because it meant coming to my home territory and speaking to a lot of people who knew me and knew my family personally. But we prepared, prayed, and anticipated God's blessing. The meetings took place for a full week, every evening from Sunday through Saturday. There was a full house, standing room only, at every session during the day and every night. People came to the altar to renew and to make new commitments to Jesus. This was an exciting event. It made me realize that God can use a willing though inexperienced evangelist when He chooses to do so.

An interesting sidebar was that I was invited by some of the leaders of a new congregation that was about to start holding services, Northview Community Church, to come to Abbotsford and be their pastor. I had just started my ministry at Visalia and thought it highly inappropriate to start negotiations for a job with a different church at that time. But I kept this invitation in the back of my mind.

In the Community

A significant ministry with the police department in Visalia took shape in the first two years of my ministry there. Apparently some members of the police department had had a party, and some unsavory things had taken place at this event. The result was that the police chief was considering firing a large number of officers.

Jim German, who was a police officer from our church, had not been involved in the improper activity. He came to see me, and we prayed about what we could do to deal with this situation redemptively. I challenged him to invite the police officers who had been caught in this impropriety to come for a breakfast meeting in a local restaurant. I was surprised when about twenty-five police officers showed up. We didn't get around to eating; coffee was all that we had. I said to the men, "I'll speak for you if you will come and study the Bible with me. I'll guarantee that you will see things that you have not seen before, and you will be exposed to the truth that will make a difference in your life." To make a long story short, the chief of police withdrew his threat to fire the officers, and we began our Bible studies. After six years of weekly Bible studies at 6:00 a.m. on Tuesday mornings, a score of police officers changed their lifestyles. Many had become Christians, others had been baptized, and others were just open to the Lord again. Suddenly we discovered the power of God coming to Neighborhood Church. The mayor, the city manager, the president of a local college, the county school superintendent, and the chief of police were all making Neighborhood their home church.

About the middle of this time, at an awards banquet around Christmas, I gave a brief address. To my surprise, the police honored me by presenting me with an official police badge as the chaplain of the police department. The police chief told me that this badge could get me out of tickets—and in following years this proved to be true!

Our children were all busy in school. Murray was at Immanuel High School, playing football and basketball and playing drums in the In To Focus Band. Bob was also at Immanuel, enjoying drama, baseball, and football. Dave was at Green Acres Junior High School, enjoying baseball and many other sports. Karla was enjoying elementary school. We made it a practice to be at all the kids' school events, so we could celebrate with them and be with them through all the ups and downs of their lives. We tried to make Friday evenings family nights. We would go out to see a movie or an event together or simply go out to eat. These were good times. The kids enjoyed being together as a family.

Carol began working as a teacher's aide at Washington Elementary School in Visalia. The teachers were highly appreciative of her skills in teaching, and the children gained confidence in their school work.

Broader Church Work

I was also involved in the wider Mennonite Brethren Church in the US. I served two terms as moderator of the Pacific District Conference of Mennonite Brethren Churches, which included Washington, Oregon, Oklahoma, and Arizona. A highlight of this time was the building of a new gymnasium and multi-purpose center at Fresno Pacific College (now Fresno Pacific University), which was owned by the Conference. The Conference also planted a number of new churches.

I also served for thirteen years on the board of Mennonite Brethren Biblical Seminary. During this time, we established a seminary presence on the campus of Fresno Pacific College. We also obtained accreditation for the graduate program at the seminary, and built a faculty that prepared people for ministry in our constituency. I served as chairman of the board in my last term, while I was in Visalia.

In Neighborhood Church, we were moving from leadership by a church council to leadership by a board of elders. We studied the subject of eldership in the Scriptures, and, after much discussion, we moved to the eldership model, which made each elder responsible for carrying out specific ministries and for preparing others for ministry. It was not a matter of administrating departments and programs, but of leading people to follow Christ in their lifestyles and with their gifts.

We also built a new sanctuary that seated 500 people, but soon realized that we had some limitations with the three-acre property that we were on. After Carol and I left Visalia, the church bought a new piece of property, and weekly attendance has now reached about 1200. It's good to see a church continue to thrive after the senior pastor has finished his tour of duty.

A church that is urban needs to pay particular attention to building relationships. So we divided the church into small groups, which met monthly and were led by deacons and elders. We also had annual family camps for the entire congregation. These were always memorable times where we got to know each other and encouraged each other in the faith. Beyond that, we had things like a "homecoming" event in the fall, church picnics, and ice cream socials. The relational quality of the church was such that it attracted people to come and participate and be part of the congregation.

As far as Carol and I and our family were concerned, we were going to stay in Visalia a long time and help carry out the ministry of the church. However, God had other things in mind. After eight years of ministry, we discovered the best was yet to be.

Chapter 10
A Prophet comes Home

*"All Scripture is God-breathed and is useful for teaching, rebuking,
correcting and training in righteousness, so that the man of God may
be thoroughly equipped for every good work."*
2 Timothy 3:16-17

I had grown up in Abbotsford and knew the territory very well. I had an inkling that I might someday come back into the community and serve as pastor. The Lord had given me a premonition that this might be something that would happen for me down the road.

In 1987, I was in a restaurant in Visalia enjoying a meal when Don Voth, the leader of Northview Community Church in Abbotsford, appeared. We greeted each other, and the conversation soon came around to what was happening at Northview. He said he would like to put my name forward to be the senior pastor at the church. I listened carefully and was excited with him about all the good things that were happening. The church had purchased ten acres of property, the church was doing well financially, and attendance was running at over 400 people for the weekend services.

But moving to Abbotsford just didn't fit into our family's schedule right then. We had three sons at Fresno Pacific College, our daughter Karla was in high school, and Carol was working at a school as an instructional aide. I also felt that my ministry was critical for Neighborhood Church at this point. We had been there for seven years and needed to finish the projects that we had begun.

Don listened carefully and was understanding. He said he would call back in the fall and see how we were feeling then. I can't say that we gave it much thought over the summer, but from time to time we prayed that the Lord would send the right pastor to Northview. We did not feel any drawing towards the church ourselves.

November came, and Don called. After a considerable amount of discussion, I made it clear to him that we were not open to a call at that time.

That night I could not sleep. I kept waking up and feeling the Lord tugging at my heart. Carol and I both felt that God was drawing us to be open to this call. I called Don back and said something like this: "I'm sure that you have considered someone else since your call to us, since we gave you a final 'No.' However, if you are open to reconsider, we would be open to reconsider as well." After some more discussion, Don said to me, "If you would have said 'No,' we would have called you again next month." This seemed like a strong indicator that God was bringing us together.

We gathered our four children around us and began to pray and seek God's face concerning their participation in this move. The three boys, Murray, Bob, and Dave, said that they would remain in the US, go to school, and find a job. Karla wasn't sure what to do; she would be graduating from high school in the spring. They each said that they were seeing this as God's will for Mom and Dad, but it did not involve them because they were adults and would be making their own decisions. Karla did decide to move to British Columbia with us; however, this transition was not an easy one, with our family being divided for the first time. We did have the assurance that God was leading us.

Although this move meant leaving our three sons in the Fresno area, it also meant moving closer to our parents. In all the years of our ministry, we had lived away from them. My mother had been widowed, and Carol's dad was dealing with cancer. So, responding to the call from Northview was also God's design for us to be close to our parents.

I did quite a bit of reflecting on what I would like to focus on when we began our ministry at Northview. There were four things that I wanted for the church in the first months of our ministry here.

1. Biblical Preaching

First, I wanted us to take seriously that "All Scripture is God-breathed and is useful for teaching, rebuking, correcting and training in righteousness, so that the man of God may be thoroughly equipped for every good work." (2 Timothy 3:16-17) I drove this point home when I preached my first sermon at Northview in July 1988. With a stack of Bibles on a table at the front of the church, I quoted from each one the verses I had found which had had profound meaning for me over the first forty-seven years of my life. I told stories of what each Bible had meant to me, all the way from the first German-language Bible my mother had used to lead me to Christ, through the various Bibles that I had learned from when I was going through times of rebellion, times of growth, and times of decision. I said that we would be studying the Scriptures to prepare us for whatever God would call us to do at Northview. It was the Scriptures that were powerful, the Scriptures that would teach us, the Scriptures that we would learn from together.

2. Friendship Evangelism

Second, I wanted us to learn friendship evangelism. By this I meant "doing, being, and telling the gospel in the power of the Spirit and leaving the results for God." I presented the challenge that every person at Northview, at some time in their lifetime, would go on a mission assignment. I could feel a sense of excitement moving over the members of the church when this was spoken out to them. I said that the church would give an opportunity for each person to go if they were led to do a mission assignment. That vision is still being carried out today.

To help with the friendship evangelism, we determined that we would organize big community events that would be an opportunity for our members to invite their neighbors and friends. So we had a "homecoming" extravaganza in September and Christmas Eve services—five of them—and an Easter musical. We found that after these big events, there were always a lot of new people at church who were searching for the Lord; many of them found Northview to be a place where they could come to learn and be integrated into a Christian community.

3. Spiritual Gifting

Third, I wanted very much for the church members to have a sense of their individual gifting and of the gifting the Lord had given us as a congregation. So, for the first six weeks of my ministry there, I dedicated Sunday nights to be a gift discovery time. I taught the biblical basis for gifts, the results of gifts, and the joy of using gifts both individually and in connection with the rest of the body of Christ. It was the apostle Paul who said that the Holy Spirit "gave some to be apostles, some to be prophets, some to be evangelists, and some to be pastors and teachers, to prepare God's people for works of service." (Ephesians 4:11-12) In other words, for the church to be a serving church, it would need to be filled with the Holy Spirit and to be aware of the gifting that the Holy Spirit had given for that divine work. It was exciting to think of the endowment of the Holy Spirit resting upon us individually and as a church.

4. A Gifted Staff

Fourth, I had found that building a gifted staff was absolutely critical to have a healthy growing church—staff who were endowed by the Holy Spirit with the appropriate gifts, staff who were obedient to the Lord, and staff who enjoyed serving together. As we called more staff over the years, we discovered that God had often prepared people to join the staff before we ever contacted them. This added a dynamic dimension to calling new staff. We staffed a strong children's program, youth ministry, young adults ministry, adults ministry, and missions ministry. Over the years, staffing our church also presented some challenges, which, together with the leadership, we worked through.

The Story

I was sitting in a restaurant in Abbotsford one Saturday morning, reading my Bible and watching people. Quite suddenly, two gentlemen, about thirty-five years old, entered the restaurant and seemed to be searching for someone. When they caught my eye, they immediately moved towards me and asked if they could sit in the booth with me. Being one who enjoyed all that happens in restaurants, I gladly agreed. They asked me what I did for a living. When I said I was a pastor, they looked at each other with surprise and delight. They said they had a story to tell. They talked; I listened. They said they were both carpenters and were on the way to Vancouver for a convention on the weekend. Driving west down Number 1 Highway, they sensed the Lord telling them that they had a special ministry to perform that day and they should prepare themselves for it. They were going to meet someone, and they were supposed to bless that person when they met him. When they came up to the Clearbrook interchange, the Holy Spirit directed them to turn right, so they turned right and kept driving. Somehow they had a sense that God would direct them when to turn next. Sure enough, when they reached South Fraser Way, the Holy Spirit impressed upon them that they should turn right; they turned right. This had never happened to them before, they said; this was a new experience. As they drove up South Fraser Way, they passed a number of buildings. And then the Holy Spirit impressed upon them that they should stop at the International House of Pancakes. So they parked in the parking lot and came in with great anticipation. They were delighted to find someone sitting reading the Bible, and they had the confidence to come and talk to me.

We chatted some more, and they said, "We have a task to do. We will do it, and then we will continue on our way."

I asked, "What is your task?"

They said, "The Holy Spirit has asked us to bless you. You have been called by the Lord for a special task to your generation. We are here to bless you and assure you that God is going to do everything

He wants through you. Don't be afraid to go to the ends of the earth to do whatever God has asked you to do." Then they laid hands on me and prayed over me.

When I got home, I told Carol the story. We were both surprised, and we weren't sure exactly what to make of the incident, but it was certainly encouraging. The next Sunday, the services were fuller than ever. The main sanctuary was overflowing, and the youth center was filled with an overflow crowd. I preached the message, and the two friends who had met me in the restaurant were sitting in the front row. I could sense them praying on behalf of the church and the power of the Holy Spirit coming in. I have never met those men again, but I have no doubt in my mind that they were sent by the Lord to bless us. I made up my mind that I should encourage my friends and myself to do as these men did, to bless people as often as God impresses the inclination upon us. It makes a huge difference. The best is yet to be.

Chapter 11
Growing a Joy-Filled Family

"Rejoice in the Lord always. I will say it again: Rejoice!"
Philippians 4:4

*"Consider it pure joy, my brothers, whenever you face trials of many
kinds, because you know that the testing of your faith develops
perseverance. Perseverance must finish its work so that you may be
mature and complete, not lacking anything."*
James 1:2-4

We know that family is a joy and also a test. All the dimensions of a person's patience and excitement are put on display in this intimate, caring relationship. Consider these two passages of Scripture, which almost seem to be saying opposite things:

"Rejoice in the Lord always. I will say it again: Rejoice!" (Philippians 4:4) Here is a call to rejoice "in" the Lord. This sounds like a life of consistent joy, a happiness that doesn't stop!

"Consider it pure joy, my brothers, when you face trials of many kinds, because you know that the testing of your faith develops perseverance. Perseverance must finish its work so that you may be mature and complete, not lacking anything." (James 1:2-4)

Put together, these verses tell us that we should rejoice in the Lord always—in the good times and when we face all kinds of trials. That covers the whole gamut of life.

There are a number of things that Carol and I did with each one of our children as they entered this world and walked alongside us into life. First, we celebrated their births. I can still see the glow on Carol's face when each one of our children was born. She had given birth to a life, a gift of God, someone to be treasured! I had the same excitement and delight in seeing our children born healthy and ready to enter life by God's grace.

Dedicated in Church

Each one of our children was dedicated in church before the Lord. This act of dedication does not save anyone, but it did say that we as parents were committing ourselves to raise this child in the knowledge of God and the Scriptures.

Every time that one of the children celebrated a birthday, we made it a special event—all the way from making a personalized cake to getting the right gift. Beyond that, we always tried to make the celebration a spiritual experience as well, with prayer and thanksgiving for the gift that this particular child was to us from the Lord.

A Christian Bar Mitzvah

We came up with this idea from a magazine article which we read. In the Jewish community, all boys, at age thirteen, go through a Bar Mitzvah experience, which includes reading and memorizing various Scriptures. (Girls go through a similar Bat Mitzvah experience.) We thought we would adapt this custom to our contemporary age, but it was still a very meaningful custom for us. When each of our children turned thirteen, we took them out for a date night to the finest restaurant we could find. We let them choose whatever they wished off the menu—ouch! Then we took time to let them know how much we loved them and how much we appreciated having them as our children. We also presented them with a new Bible.

All of our children had received the Lord by the time they were thirteen, so we had them repeat back to us their concept of what salvation meant for them at this point. We assured them of our prayers and also assured them that there would be struggles and strained relationships because that's the way it is, but that we would never, ever stop loving them.

The Bar Mitzvah was an occasion for us to tell our children that they were moving into a new phase. As parents, we would be changing from exercising leadership by giving commands to exercising leadership by giving counsel. We would be giving our children more opportunity to make decisions as they showed themselves mature enough to do so. This is where most tensions arise between parents and children, isn't it? How do parents give over authority to their sons and daughters— and do it without arousing some riotous argument? But we are to consider even this challenge pure joy, because it is another step in them becoming "mature and complete, not lacking in anything."

Graduation

High school graduation was a rite of passage as well. I will never forget Karla's graduation experience in Reedley, California. She was walking across the stage dressed in a beautiful gown and ready to accept her credentials when suddenly her three brothers stood up in the auditorium and shouted, "Praise the Lord!" There was a moment of embarrassment but also a moment of pride as Karla recognized that her brothers had chosen to draw attention to her.

We gave each of our children a thousand dollars on their graduation, which they could use either for making a trip or for making a down payment on a car.

Then Comes the Groom

I had the privilege of officiating at the wedding of each of our children. We had prayed that each of them would find the life's partner that God had prepared for them. What a joy to celebrate the answers to our prayers! Years later, we are now enjoying these four families, including twelve wonderful grandchildren. Murray and Holly live in Portland, Oregon, with their children, Noah and Avery. Bob and JoAnn, with their children, Karis, Connor, and Elisa, are at Sugar Pine Christian Camp in Oakhurst, California. Dave and Michelle live in Abbotsford, B.C., with their children, Jonas, Jack, and Jase. Karla and Menno reside in Abbotsford with their children, Karli, Riley, Maya, and Brody. Family has always been a high priority for us and still is today.

Life goes on. We moved from celebration to celebration, and from test to test. When all is said and done, love is the greatest. It is a mark of being in touch with God. We pray that all of our children's marriages will remain holy and blessed.

A Picture of God's Grace

Carol and I were sitting in the living room reading the paper one evening when Karla came to join us. She looked somewhat drawn and nervous. Suddenly she said, "I have something to tell you, Mom and Dad." We waited, we waited, and we waited some more. Finally, after about a half hour of waiting, she blurted out, "I'm pregnant!"

Nothing could have surprised us more than that. We tried to give Karla some initial assurances of our love and care for her and tell her that we would help to see her through. But where would we start?

I mentioned to Carol that I had had coffee that day with Lorne Welwood and he had told me that his wife Ann had founded Hope Services, a ministry that helped young women who were dealing with unwanted pregnancies. We quickly gave them a call, and they came over. The next hour and a half we spent together was one of the most meaningful times we have ever had with a counselor. They told us and Karla that we should not try to solve the crisis that day, that we should trust the Lord in this situation, and that we should take it one step at a time.

The next day, we called the church elders together and shared what had happened. I offered my resignation as senior pastor, feeling that the church should have an option to decide whether I should stay or not. The next Sunday night, we had a communion service, and I stood up and shared what had happened in our family. I told the congregation that Karla had confessed before the elders and was ready to follow the discipline of submitting to the Lord.

The elders then got up and asked the congregation, "What should we do?" A motion was made that a vote should be taken as to whether I should stay on as senior pastor. After prayer and some discussion, the vote was taken. The result was 100 percent that I should stay on as senior pastor. It just broke me up to have that kind of confidence placed in me in the midst of difficulties. My heart and Carol's melted together in the church like never before. It was an amazing moment, painful but therapeutic!

For the next eight months, Karla came to church each weekend and often sat with me until it was time for me to preach. We demonstrated our oneness in the Lord and our oneness as father and daughter. When the child was born, Karla was given the full right to make her own decision as to whether she would give the child up for adoption or care for the child herself. After having a number of counseling sessions with Ann and carefully considering her options, she chose to keep her baby, Karli Marisa. All of this went on in the view of the whole congregation. It was a powerful message. There were a lot of people who were in a similar situation; they called us and asked for counsel on how we had dealt with it. They needed a model to follow. Karla and I also spoke at a number of banquets, telling our story and helping to raise funds for this kind of ministry.

Carol and I also went to each one of our family members and told the story to them. We also spoke to our close friends about the situation, so that everyone would know what had happened and how things were going in our lives. That which could have been a murmuring in the community became a story of blessing. Hallelujah! We found that God could bring joy into our family when we followed His ways even through difficult times. Today we are so blessed to have Karli in our family.

Our family has been a great blessing to us. But the best is yet to be.

Chapter 12
Following the Acts Model

"You will receive power when the Holy Spirit comes on you; and you will be my witnesses in Jerusalem, and in all Judea and Samaria, and to the ends of the earth."
Acts 1:8

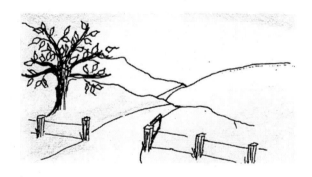

Early on in my ministry, God impressed upon me the principle that it should be a natural thing for a church or individual to begin at home and arrive at some distance from home in terms of being a witness for Christ. This is described in Acts 1:8: "You will receive power when the Holy Spirit comes on you; and you will be my witnesses in Jerusalem, and in all Judea and Samaria, and to the ends of the earth." These are words of instruction from the Holy Spirit to the church. It is interesting that when we follow His guidance, He directs our paths, in a progression from close to home to the farthest corners of the earth. This is the experience that we had in Northview and the other churches that we pastored. I also found it to be true in the ministry that God gave me personally, which included mission journeys to Russia, Japan, and the Philippines.

1. A Journey to Russia

In 1993, the Mennonite Brethren mission board requested that I go to Russia and spend some time teaching in St. Petersburg Christian University in the area of evangelism and Christian leadership. A good friend of mine, Garry Schmidt, decided to join in on this adventure to a part of the world that was unfamiliar to us. I was glad to have him along because we had been friends for many years and worked well together. It was exciting to read up on the area and prepare lessons that we felt would help make a difference.

We flew out from Seattle and into Lithuania, where there was a school set up to train men and women to be tentmaking pastors. Garry and I taught Christian leadership and spiritual formation every afternoon for one week. The class consisted of about twenty students in their late teens and early twenties. It was exciting to be with these vigorous young students who wanted to know the Scriptures and also how to make a living on the side. It was exciting to give them firsthand instruction from the Bible on how to be a leader. They were good thinkers and hard workers who will make a big difference in the coming generation.

After a week of study with them, we boarded the train to St. Petersburg, a trip of several hundred miles, so we could kick back and relax. The train car that we were in was brand new, made in a factory in Germany. We had bunk beds, so we looked forward to a restful sleep.

About two or three in the morning, there was a rattling at our door and some gruff voices trying to get our attention. We hesitated a bit, but the noise increased. Someone was banging a rifle against our door. When we finally answered the door, we saw a military officer together with the train conductor. They wanted to see our passports and visas and asked us to read all kinds of papers that were necessary to enter Russia. The banging of a gunstock against the door in the middle of the night didn't give us much reason to believe that everything was okay, but it introduced us to a community which was used to living under the strong hand of a dictatorship. It felt like a communist country all over again. We finally got all of our papers straightened out and went back to sleep.

After the drama of the night, it was exciting to see the countryside as we flew down the tracks. On one occasion, for about twenty-five miles we saw scores of small shacks nestled along the river. We were told that the Russian folk built these small, inexpensive shanties and came here in summer to do their relaxation and vacationing. They also grew vegetables and raised small animals so they could have food for winter. Very interesting.

We arrived at the St. Petersburg train station and found it filled with people from every ethnic group you can imagine. We were to be met by someone from the Christian university. We waded through the crowd to the place where we thought we were supposed to meet our driver, but there was no one to be found. The place teemed with people, and we could hardly find a clear spot to sit down. After we had walked the circuit three or four times, we finally gave up and just sat down and waited. Sure enough, after several hours, a familiar voice called us by name. I looked up, and, to my surprise, it was someone I hadn't seen for a long time—Dwight Aikin, my former Hebrew teacher at seminary. Along with his son, he had taken his time checking out the train station.

Dwight took us to the university and put us up in a student residence. Then we met with the leadership and the teaching team to arrange our classes. Our main teaching would be two hours every evening after supper at the end of a normal teaching day. The sessions that we would conduct were attended by about twenty-five students in a teaching theatre. I taught for an hour on the spiritual leadership of a minister, and then Garry taught for an hour on spiritual formation.

During the daytime, we would take turns entering various classrooms and sharing insights and responding to questions. These young pastors were eager to learn the secrets of ministry and had a passion for the people of Russia. Russia had many small Baptist churches, which had struggled to survive under difficult situations for decades. These young pastors had grown up during the communist era and had learned their skills under a very different situation. They had little understanding of modern ministry and needed instruction on how to draw younger pastors in and develop effective ministry teams. It was exciting to be able to offer them some new insights from the West that they probably hadn't seen before and that they thought they could apply to their situation. These one-on-one encounters were the most enjoyable part of the time Garry and I spent in the university. To be encouraged and to receive encouragement was delightful. Our prayer was that we would be more equipped for ministry as a result of our being with them.

We were put up in the student quarters and had a studio for ourselves. It was not fancy but convenient, with amenities like showers and washbasins. We had a surprise on Wednesday morning when we couldn't get the hot water to work in the shower; only cold water was coming out of the tap. We checked with the school janitor to see what was the matter and found out that the Russian government had made an arbitrary decision that on April 15 every spring the hot water would be turned off for the rest of the spring and summer. For the rest of the days that we were there, it would be cold showers or nothing! We did not look forward to taking our showers, no matter how necessary they were.

When you speak in a foreign country, you have to work through a translator. The first translator I had was only nineteen years old, but he understood language and how to translate quickly. The second day, however, the translator I had was slow. From time to time, he would call me to the side, and we would have a discussion on what the meaning of a particular word was. To be a translator was a highly profitable occupation in Russia. A doctor would make seventy-five dollars a month, while a translator could make at least a hundred dollars a month.

We took the subway to downtown and also took a taxi from time to time. One of the favorite places downtown was a Wendy's hamburger restaurant. There was nothing else like it in Russia. There was a military person at every entrance and exit door to prevent theft. During our time in St. Petersburg, we took the opportunity to tour the Hermitage Museum, and we were also culturally enriched by attending *The Nutcracker* ballet.

After seven days, our ministry came to an end. Garry and I had tested our wings in terms of working together as a team. It was an exhilarating experience, and both of us were richer because of it. We flew back, stopping in Denmark for a day's rest before continuing on to Seattle. We were glad that there was a washer and dryer in our hotel in Denmark so we could clean ourselves up somewhat before seeing our families at home.

2. A Journey to Japan

The Mennonite Brethren churches in Japan had asked for a representative of the Mennonite Brethren church in North America to come to be the speaker at their national convention in 1998 and also teach a seminar in the area of Christian leadership. It fit into my schedule, so I accepted the assignment. We had at one point applied to be missionaries in Japan, so I had a special interest in seeing what this place looked like in person.

I was picked up by a good brother at the airport, and we made our way to a restaurant. He said that I needed to have some Japanese sushi so I could be strong and be ready for the assignment. I said that I enjoyed sushi, but it turned out to have too much "life" for me—the fish was still wiggling when I was swallowing it, and I felt a little overwhelmed. We had a good laugh and struck up a friendship.

The Mennonite Brethren churches in Japan had a retreat center where they conducted conferences and retreats. There was an apartment upstairs for the visiting speaker. I brought my suitcase in and looked around, and was amazed that there was no chair in the place and no desk either—just a big, soft cushion on the floor. I guess I was meant to be Japanese and learn how to do my work on the floor rather than at a desk. Working this way was quite a cultural adjustment.

The conference began with Sunday morning and evening sessions, at which I spoke. When I entered the sanctuary, the usher advised me that I needed to take off my shoes and put on a pair of slippers. When they finally found a pair my size, I followed the usher up the aisle to the stage, where they took the slippers from my feet and gave me another pair of slippers, especially designated for being on the preaching stage. But that wasn't all. Next I had to switch to a third pair of slippers that were used for standing behind the pulpit when I preached.

I stood there before I preached and looked into the audience, overwhelmed with the fact that these were my brothers and sisters. I had never met them, but we had the same Lord, the same Savior, the same Messiah. I sensed the Holy Spirit come upon me as I preached the Word.

There were about eight congregations that had gathered for this special celebration Sunday. After the morning service, there was a potluck dinner, with many tables filled with all sorts of sushi. I was amazed that there was also a table that had Kentucky fried chicken, which was the most popular of all.

A professor from Dallas Theological Seminary was teaching a section on eschatology, and I would be teaching a section on the church and New Testament leadership. We had a good time exchanging notes and visiting with one another during the five-day conference. Every evening, he spoke for an hour, and I spoke for an hour, followed by a question and answer session.

The leader of the retreat center told me that one of the problems they faced was that it was hard to attract men to church. Church involvement was more a feminine thing than a masculine thing in Japan. However, there were a good number of young men who had been trained to be ministers at the retreat center. The churches were impressed by their dedication and the direction they were taking the churches.

One of the pastors said, "I hope you don't drop the 'Heidebrecht bomb' when you speak tonight."

I said, "What do you mean by the 'Heidebrecht bomb'?"

He said, "Well, that you would say something that is so out of the realm of our experience that it feels like a bomb when you drop it on us."

"Give me an example," I said.

He said, "For example, when you say that you allow lay people to do a baptism service, that is something that is out of our experience. We feel that it needs to be an ordained minister who does that."

We had a good laugh about that, and I teased them about the bomb that I was going to drop in the future.

The conference was well received, and I received considerable affirmation. It was a whole new world that I experienced in Japan. It felt like "the ends of the earth" that Jesus had talked about.

3. A Journey to the Philippines

When I was a member of the board of the Evangelical Fellowship of Canada, we were asked by the World Evangelical Fellowship (WEF, now World Evangelical Alliance) to host a conference in Abbotsford for evangelicals from around the world. There was a meeting of about fifteen people who had expressed interest in working with the Evangelical Fellowship of Canada to organize this event. I became the chairperson of that hosting committee. We were responsible for arranging ground transportation, raising financial support, and a host of other administrative details. The person we worked with most closely in the planning was Dr. Jun Vencer from the Philippines, who was international director of the WEF. We worked well together. The sessions were held in the spacious Central Heights Mennonite Brethren Church in Abbotsford for a full week in May 1997. The church was full, with standing room only.

Everything went very well during the conference. The Holy Spirit was very evidently working in the lives of people. There was a lot of passion for world evangelization, and a lot of helpful insights shared on how this should be done. By Wednesday, at a meeting of Canadian representatives, a decision was made that an Abbotsford person should speak at the convention as well. It was a last moment decision, but one that was considered significant because we had put our hearts and souls into preparing for the conference. I was humbled when they decided that I should address the conference on the final night. As I prayed, the Holy Spirit gave me a message even before I opened the Bible to search for a text. The thought that God put into my heart was that there needed to be a humbling of the nations one to another and that this could be shown most clearly by the washing of feet, because we show the greatest amount of love when we do this. So, I arranged with Dr. Vencer that I would wash his feet in front of the whole delegation. When the night came, I gave a brief introduction to the biblical practice of foot washing, as well as the significant role that Dr. Vencer had in keeping the organization pure and holy by God's grace. Then I took a bowl of water and a towel and washed his feet. After I was through, Dr. Vencer called a man from the audience and began washing his feet. The man whose feet he was washing was a pastor from Rwanda whose sons had been killed in the recent civil war. Dr. Vencer told the man's story while he was washing his feet, and the whole group of people that were gathered were moved very deeply. I went to the microphone and said that all those who wanted to humble themselves before the Lord so that He could work through us in a greater way should come to the altar and pray together. I had hardly spoken the first sentence of the invitation when people began streaming to the front. It was amazing how people were able to share their brokenness before the Lord. People were praying, crying, rejoicing, and confessing together. It was a wonderful conclusion to the conference.

After the conference was over, Dr. Vencer asked me if I would come to the Philippines and preach the Word at their national convention as I had at the conference in Abbotsford. I said, "Yes." I recall the euphoric feeling I had in my heart as later that year I flew to the Philippines and was able to share the Word at their national gathering.

The result was that Dr. Vencer and I became good friends. He expressed the wish that I would join him on the WEF executive. However, this time I said, "No." I was a pastor, and I needed to remain a pastor and resume the calling God had given me.

Canada

There were other opportunities to make a national impact. When I returned to Canada, the Evangelical Fellowship of Canada was developing a team of people who would go to Ottawa once or twice a year to minister to the political leaders of our nation. Eighteen leaders from some of the larger churches in our Canadian constituency were chosen for this assignment. This group had an organizational meeting in Vancouver. Barry Bowater, a man who had done a lot of work in the nation's capital, was chosen to be executive secretary, and I was elected chairperson. It was an enriching time as these leading pastors from across the nation spent time together and shared ideas of how we could impact our nation with the gospel and also strengthen our Members of Parliament for the responsibilities that were theirs.

Our first meeting included a banquet for any Members of Parliament who were interested, and fifteen or sixteen Members of Parliament attended. I addressed the gathering on what it means to be a Christian in our nation today.

We had a separate opportunity to visit with Prime Minister Jean Chretien. We introduced ourselves to him, and he introduced himself to us by saying that his name means "Christian."

As well, we met with Paul Martin, who later had a very short term as Prime Minister of Canada.

During these years, I also had the privilege of being part of a small gathering that met with Prime Minister Stephen Harper. He openly confessed his faith in Christ. We laid hands on him and prayed for wisdom for him as he led our country. He is a man who is touching people around the world, and we had a chance to reach out and touch him by God's Spirit.

Our visit with the top leaders in Canada impressed upon us the fact that they need a lot of prayer and encouragement. They have so many responsibilities, and they can hardly do the work right without having the Lord by their side.

These were exciting opportunities, but the best is yet to be.

Chapter 13
The Parkinson's Factor

"The king's heart is in the hand of the LORD;
he directs it like a watercourse wherever he pleases."
Proverbs 21:1

It was the beginning of January 2002. I was well prepared for a weekend of messages focusing on the new year in a positive way. I had recently had to spend a longer time and more energy preparing my sermons, and I wasn't sure what the problem was. I assumed I was tired or needed some advice in public speaking. It was Saturday night, and we were going into the first of our four weekend services. The music went well, and the prayers were powerful. Everything was going well until it was time for me to come up onto the platform and speak. I slipped on the stage, and I sensed a current of negative energy flowing through me. It was almost as if I was having a panic attack. But I was a professional speaker, so, with a prayer on my breath and a smile on my face, I decided to go ahead and share what the Lord had laid on my heart. About twenty minutes into the message, I again had this panic-like feeling. I fought it for about ten minutes and felt that it was a losing battle. I announced that we would close the service early today, and I told the congregation something that they were already aware of, that I wasn't making much sense in my speech this evening. I asked individuals to just sit and pray, or leave, or do whatever they wished to do, and we would see what the Lord would do at the next service.

I sat down in the front row, and several elders came and laid hands on me and prayed over me. Others just stayed in the background and prayed. It was a funny feeling knowing that I had just stopped preaching when I was supposed to be declaring the Word.

One of the staff standing nearby asked if he could do anything.

I said, "Yes. Give me some insight as to whether I should preach at the second service tonight."

He thought for a few moments, and then he said that he had always heard that when a rider fell off his horse, he should get back on as soon as possible and ride again, or else he might lose his ability to ride.

That made sense to me! So, after a short rest and a drink of water, I went back on stage. I got through the second service, and the third and fourth on Sunday morning, and everything went well.

But the elders were not satisfied to just leave what had happened; they were concerned about my well-being. After a battery of tests, my doctor declared me healthy and said there was nothing outwardly problematic in terms of my health.

Next I went to see a psychologist. Interestingly, he suggested that I should feel free to come in the back door, so people who knew me wouldn't be embarrassed about me coming to see a psychologist. I assured him that it didn't bother me and that research was research. He made an appointment to see me again. He was concerned that I was overworked and that it was having an effect on my life, but he wasn't sure.

The next doctor I went to see was Dr. Tony Constantino, a neurologist in Abbotsford. He asked me some basic questions about my work and other things, and then he asked me to stand. He gave my chest a push with his hand. To my surprise, I stumbled and almost fell down. After I regained my balance, he asked me to stand again and gave me another push. This time I was a little stronger, but I still ended up on the floor with one knee on the ground. After a few more observation tests, he took his dictaphone and began to dictate notes regarding the visit. I was totally stunned when I heard him say, "The patient has Parkinson's disease." Parkinson's disease! What was this? I had hardly heard of the disease, and I was certainly not prepared to be labeled as a person having that disease. For the next few weeks, I went in to see Dr. Constantino regularly until he had nailed the diagnosis down. He shared with me some of the symptoms of Parkinson's disease.

Parkinson's is more common over the age of fifty-five but can occur in younger and older people, and is equally common in men and women. Here are some symptoms:

- *trembling limbs when at rest*
- *muscle rigidity*
- *slowness of movement*
- *difficulty with balance and walking*
- *reduced volume and clarity of speech*
- *difficulty with refined movements such as handwriting*

Research is in progress to determine possible causes of Parkinson's, but so far there has been no breakthrough. Researchers do know that when dopamine levels fall below fifty percent, the symptoms of Parkinson's appear. Today I take two dopamine pills every four hours.

Hearing God's Voice

Having been called by God to the work of being a minister, I had always dreamt of "riding off into the sunset" while still passionately preaching and shepherding a church. Now, with the diagnosis of Parkinson's disease, every day pulled me back to my life verse, "My grace is sufficient for you, for my power is made perfect in weakness." (2 Corinthians 12:9)

We had a sabbatical scheduled for the coming summer. The leadership of Northview Church suggested we take it earlier—and they came alongside us with encouragement and a generous gift of a trip to Hawaii. Although our plans for the future had changed, we knew God's plan for us was always good and could be trusted.

Carol and I spent two weeks in Hawaii, enjoying a time of relaxation and reflection. We decided to accept the position the church offered us as an associate pastor working in the area of prayer and discipleship. After fifteen years as senior pastor of Northview, I was able to spend another seven years as associate pastor. The last few years, I served part time, still using my gift of encouragement.

Over the past thirty years, I have journaled almost every day. The discipline has proved to be a major source of strength and daily encouragement in my walk with God. I have had many opportunities to share the insights I have received and have been able to mentor scores of others to join me in this spiritual discipline. Out of this, and with strong encouragement from others, I wrote the book *Hearing God's Voice*, which was published by Cook Communications Ministries in 2007.

Northview, for several years, had hosted the Alpha course, a proven tool for evangelism. Our concern as leaders was to provide the next step for individuals to move beyond Alpha in their spiritual growth. We were made aware of the ministry that Holy Trinity Brompton Church, under the leadership of Nicky Gumbel in London, England, was accomplishing. That church was hosting a seminar to introduce attenders to "pastorates," where individuals could experience a caring atmosphere along with solid Bible teaching. Frank and Esther Martens and Carol and I spent a week attending the seminar and learning firsthand how pastorates worked in that church parish. This experience helped to lay the groundwork so that we could train leaders and begin implementing pastorates at Northview.

Now that I am no longer on staff at Northview, we are looking forward to seeing what God has to say to us during this next stage of our lives. We are doing well, even though I am struggling with my physical well-being. We still have a general sense of God's hand on our lives. The best is yet to be. Praise the Lord!

Chapter 14
The Best Is Yet To Be

"Dear friends, now we are children of God, and what we will be has not yet been made known. But we know that when he appears, we shall be like him, for we shall see him as he is."
1 John 3:2

Looking back, one thing that has become clear is that in life often the things that we consider to be valuable may not be valuable at all. Conversely, what we think is not valuable may in fact be very valuable. We all have to make choices, and the impact of those choices is not immediately obvious. My early decision to become a follower of Jesus had a profound impact on the direction of my life, and I have been rewarded far beyond anything that I could have expected.

I had an experience several years ago that illustrates this. It was an experience for which I had to give glory to God and also to His church. An article in a local newspaper said this: "Former Northview Church senior pastor Vern Heidebrecht has officially had his name included in the book of merit that rewards people who have brought distinction to the community." The Order of Abbotsford book of merit was established by Abbotsford City Council in 2005, and I was chosen to be included in the book in 2006. The article quoted Abbotsford Mayor George Ferguson as saying that I had been a pastor for more than forty years and that I had "had to cope with the progression of Parkinson's disease." Ferguson added, "But he has maintained a positive outlook and treats his illness as an opportunity for growth."

Our theme "The best is yet to be" comes from the realization that God not only has an intense love for us but also an intense desire to give us good things. Some of those things come in this life, and some we will not receive until we meet Him face to face.

1 John 3:2 says, "Dear friends, now we are children of God, and what we will be has not yet been made known. But we know that when he appears, we shall be like him, for we shall see him as he is." It is a stretch for us to imagine that we will be like Christ when we see Him. That will be a dynamic moment when our old body, our old weaknesses and sicknesses, will all be taken away and we will be perfect like Christ. 1 Corinthians 2:9 confirms, "No eye has seen, no ear has heard, no mind has conceived what God has prepared for those who love him." Again, the Scripture uses superlative language to speak of what it is going to be like when we see Jesus. We will never have to turn back and say, "I miss the world or the things of the world." We will be complete and content in Christ. That is why we can say: The best is yet to be.

Epilogue

"To all who received him, to those who believed in his name, he gave the right to become children of God."
John 1:12

My passion has always been to introduce people to Jesus. Whether sitting in a restaurant, flying on an airplane, or preaching to my congregation, wherever I have encountered people, I have been convinced that God set up these encounters for a reason. I have found joy in conversing with people about where they were on their journey in life. Listening to their story and telling them my story became a bridge to share the good news about Jesus.

I pray the same will be true for those who have encountered my story by reading this book. I invite you to make Jesus Christ the Lord of your life. He has paid the penalty to forgive your sins on the cross, and He wants to apply that as a precious gift to your life. Listen to John 1:12: "To all who received him, to those who believed in his name, he gave the right to become children of God." If this stirs something in you, or if anything concerning my life speaks to you, you can be assured that you, too, can receive Christ into your life as Savior and Lord. You will never be sorry for making that decision. It will make a difference in your life on this earth and in your eternal destiny. God is a God of grace, ready to forgive all who come to Him. Here is a prayer that you can pray: "Dear Lord, thank You for loving me and calling me to be one of Your children. I confess my sins, and I invite You to be my Lord and Savior."

If you prayed this prayer, then you have taken the first step on your spiritual journey. Talk about it with a Christian brother or sister and commit together to grow in the Lord. It will be the greatest and most significant thing you will ever do in your life. May God bless you, and may God make your life a blessing. The best is yet to be.